Summ

Practical
Summit! by Laurie Bagley. The book is based on real life experiences that make the point. If you have a clear target of what
you want to achieve, a step-by-step plan on how to achieve
that target, and most importantly a method of managing your
mental and physical resources, then you're in position to live a
richer, fuller life. The logic is sound! The stories are compelling! What would YOU do if you absolutely knew you couldn't
fail? Reading this book may very well give you the answer.
—**R. Douglas Carter**, President, Carter International Training
and Development Company

In a world inundated with authorities on personal success and
achievement, Laurie Bagley stands above the crowd...she's an
expert! She's been there; she's done that!

Laurie shares an intimate and compelling account of what
she experienced physically, mentally and emotionally conquer-
ing the highest mountain on the planet, to stand at top of the
world and perhaps the greatest challenge of all, return safely to
live another day!

Only 20 percent of men and women today ever make a
commitment to ascend from a state of becoming to a state
of being in their lifetime. Only 1 percent will ever distinguish
themselves as Laurie Bagley, the sixth woman in the U.S. to
summit Mt. Everest. Individuals on a personal journey to
conquer fear with courage and replace doubt with certainty
will gain invaluable wisdom and inspiration reading *Summit!*. Find out what it takes to conquer your own Everest, to
stand at top of the world and put one foot in front of the other.
—**Dr. Jim Wendling**, The Wendling Group

Laurie Bagley's book uses her thrilling and terrifying journey
to the top of the world as a metaphor for life. She deftly weaves
between her adventure up Everest's North Face and down-to-
Earth life tips. It's a thrilling ride!
—**Francis Tapon**, author of *Hike Your Own Hike*

SUMMIT!

One Woman's Mount Everest Climb

Guides You to Success

Laurie Bagley

Ardenwood Books

Point Richmond, California

Library of Congress Control Number: 2010934625

A portion of the proceeds from this book support
Diane Kirwin's important charitable organization,
KIRF India. www.kirfindia.org

———————————————

Dedication

To my daughter Avriel Karseboom, who is my constant motivation, inspiration, and compass point, and to Scott Woolums, who was one of my angels on Mount Everest.

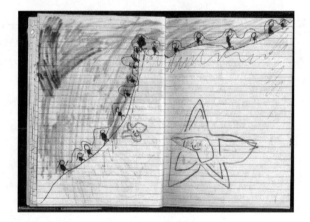

Avriel Karseboom drew this picture one week before her mother left for Everest. The drawing depicts the mountain with all the climbers. The person who has reached the top is Laurie's Sherpa; Laurie is the climber just behind him. Avriel was nine years old at the time.

Table of Contents

PART FOUR: Success One Step at a Time

Author Preface

As author of this book, I share with you my insights and tools for achieving heartfelt dreams, goals, and desires. I offer a powerful perspective for actualizing great endeavors. While success in business and sports may typically receive the most publicity and outward congratulations, I believe that the inner successes are the most profound and life changing.

My voice of experience brings wisdom from my journeys of success to assist you in identifying your dreams and creating an action plan to achieve them. I cannot do the work for you. You are the one who will put one foot in front of the other and climb the mountain of success, one step at a time, through all kinds of weather and adversity. You will then stand on top of the world, breathless with pure joy, exhilarated that you have achieved your dream.

Be open to redefining what you have considered success. Allow success to be a moment-by-moment experience and not just an end result. Understand that your success affects others. Know that any individual who commits to a goal and follows through with discipline and integrity lifts the collective human spirit.

You will receive the most benefit from this book by following the chapters in order. Claim and practice that which feels right and true for you, and then apply the lessons and action steps to reach the goals you choose to pursue. I recommend that you chart your progress in a notebook that you dedicate for your responses to the exercises at the end of each chapter. Each question, or action step, is designed to help you move forward on the path to identifying and achieving your dream or goal.

I stand with you in encouragement and in celebration, for I know and trust the journey you are embarking on. With commitment, dedicated action, and perseverance you have the potential to arrive safe and sound on top of your world.

May you be aware and enjoy the journey every step of the way.

Laurie Bagley

Acknowledgments

I would like to extend a huge thank you to my close friend and business associate Joy Von S., who laid the ground work for this book and has been one of the key people on my support team. Further, without the hours of time and energy that Victoria Song put into writing the foundation for *Summit!* I would never have been able to finish the project on my own.

I would also like to extend a huge thanks to Mary Lee Cole for her compassionate coaching while I finished the book, and to her business partner and husband David Cole for his heartfelt guidance and direction.

Thanks go to my family for their constant encouragement, particularly my parents, Don and Jean Bagley, for stretching to accomodate and accept me for who I am these past few years.

Finally, thank you to Scott Woolums for the use of his images. You can learn more about Scott's work at www.adventuresinternational.com.

Part I

Let the Journey Begin

In the next five chapters I will outline first steps for your journey to accomplish your big goal. The first consideration is identifying your dream. Once you have this you can begin the process of turning it into a goal. You will also learn how to create clarity for yourself. This requires you to examine and identify your gifts and passions. When you have clearly identified your gifts and passions, you can focus on commitment, which will support your route planning.

Commitment is the foundation of your success. You also must be doubly sure that the goal you have chosen is right for you, so you can go the distance and stay focused for the duration. And lastly, you want to make sure you are crystal clear about your "why," your reason for choosing your goal. Why have you chosen this particular goal? What about it is compelling, inspiring, and worth doing?

Commitment and perseverance brought me to the peak of my success on May 25, 2006. At approximately seven a.m. I took the last step in my journey to the pinnacle of world. The sky was blue, clear, and bright above me. A white blanket of clouds, a portent of a storm, gathered below me. From my vantage point I could see the endless peaks of the Himalayan range. The air temperature was close to minus fifteen degrees Fahrenheit with a wind chill of thirty-eight degrees below zero. I must have felt the cold somewhere in my heavily clad body. However it could not distract me from this most powerful moment. There I was standing on the small platform that is said to be the top of the world. I was graced by this powerful mountain and allowed to be one of the fortunate few to actually summit her 29,028 foot peak that glorious morning.

How did I get there? Simply, I was awake to my dream to climb Mount Everest and attempt to reach the summit. I set firm goals and took consistent, dedicated action toward that end. I did my work and invested countless hours and years that spanned the time between awakening to my dream and its actualization. Passion and purpose fueled my committed actions. It was personal, intensely personal. I was solely responsible for my accomplishments; therefore, I planned out and sharpened my focus on every detail needed to achieve the realization of my goal.

Through the pages of this book I will share with you a clear path for you to walk towards achieving your biggest accomplishments. I encourage you to recognize the greatness that resides within you. It is all too easy and sometimes quite comfortable to think that there are only a certain few who can reach great heights of achievement. But those who live their dreams are people like you, with the courage to believe and proceed.

Everything I have written in these pages is based on my personal experience. This is not theory. I have lived through years of sweat, labor, focus, and perseverance. The chapters share the truth of my experience, and this truth expresses my intention to create more joy in the world; the joy of viewing life from peak experiences, the thrill of standing on the top of the world in awe of life and wonder of the human spirit.

1 | From Ordinary to Extraordinary

"Remember, what you get by reaching your destination isn't nearly as important as what you become by reaching your goals."
—Zig Ziglar, *How to Get What You Want*

We are all extraordinary. I invite you to step out of an ordinary life and experience an extraordinary life. Through the insights in this book you will be given the opportunity to claim your dreams and the power to succeed in actualizing them. You will choose the direction you will go. I invite you to go beyond your current life, beliefs, and limitations. I invite you to claim, act on, and achieve your greatest goals.

I had the opportunity to live my dream of actually climbing and summiting Mount Everest. Admittedly this is an extraordinary accomplishment realized by few people. But my story of climbing Mount Everest serves as an inspiring metaphor for you to use as you work towards reaching your big dreams; it will remind you that big dreams are attainable. We all have metaphoric mountains to climb that lead us eventually to successfully accomplish our dreams. Your personal Mount Everest will be different from mine, but if you continue to climb towards your dream you will see the world as if from the highest peak on earth. Another metaphor that I use is "climbing gear," which refers to the tools that you need to achieve success.

I am only the sixth woman from the United States to successfully summit Mount Everest from the North Col Route, most noted for the three steps that guard the peak of this majestic mountain. The degree of exposure one is subjected to on these steps requires unstoppable courage, physical strength, and expert climbing skills. The route is hard and cold, and the lack of oxygen makes every step challenging. Because of this, the majority of climbers opt to summit from the Southern Route. The steps that I took to attain my goal included tools, skills, and strategies that are important for reaching all goals, large and small. Courageous stories from my experience appear throughout this book to inspire you to climb higher, to take another step, and to succeed in achieving your dreams

Imagine yourself standing on the top of the world, feeling your own boots and the beat of your heart. You have not only achieved your goals, you have surpassed them. What does it feel like knowing that you have succeeded? Imagine your inner guide congratulating you with "well done." This was my experience. The culmination of my eighteen month plan had paid off. Your plan also will pay off if you outline and follow realistic steps, design appropriate strategies, and develop a time line that fits your purpose.

On the summit I must have felt fatigue; however, that was not the focus of those moments, as the wave of euphoria enveloped my total being. I do recall that life seemed to be in slow motion. I experienced mental images in frames and fragments that were filled with the day-by-day, step-by-step effort of following my plan of purposeful actions. All the incremental accomplishments related to this goal over the recent years came together in a kaleidoscopic vision. I had climbed Mount Everest. I had actually done it. And now I was required to go beyond.

As I returned to the present moment, I quickly became aware that gravity was pulling on me while the altitude disoriented me. A heavy and cumbersome oxygen mask offered breathing relief, but at the same time it further weighed down any sense of freedom of movement. Of necessity my thoughts turned to the steep and dangerous descent. I needed to focus on my next goal, to arrive safely at Camp Two.

After a fleeting thirty-five minutes on the summit, our expedition advisor noticed that my oxygen was dangerously low. Initially I experienced fear; fear is the thief of energy that can rob you of life. On Mount Everest fear could take that last bit of reserve you need to stay alive. I knew fear had to be turned away. As I checked in with myself and acknowledged that my oxygen supply was limited, I consciously slowed my breathing. Then I began the process of descending as quickly as possible.

The controlled movement down the mountain brought a sense of calm that took over my body, my mind, and my breathing. I was doing exactly what I needed to do. For the next thirty minutes I concentrated on breathing as slowly as possible while exercising the practiced feelings of disciplined serenity and self-enforced focus that had been part of my training. During the descent

I thought deeply about my daughter, my community, and all that I wanted to do in my life. This gave me the motivation needed to conserve my breath, trusting that it would allow me to have a supply of oxygen until I reached the spare bottles. By the time I reached the spare oxygen bottles my tank was empty. My life had been saved in a precarious situation. I am fortunate to be alive.

How did I master these life-saving skills? My life experiences in the world of competitive sports, endurance running, adventure racing, and mountain/river guiding that led up to climbing Mount Everest taught me how to manage my time, energy, and resources. These activities helped build the skills that I needed and helped me attain the goal that I worked so hard to achieve. As the sixth woman from the United States to summit the North Col Route, I felt a sense of awe and affirmation that my process of setting goals works. You have this same opportunity to turn dreams into reality through a simple series of steps presented in the following pages. Willingness and persistence will lead you to great achievements.

People have often asked me questions such as: "Who would be crazy enough to put their life at risk and leave their family just to climb a mountain? What in the world possessed you to climb and to summit Mount Everest? What propelled you to go through the pain and discomfort that it would take to reach the summit of Mount Everest or any of the other great peaks on this planet?"

Who would take such a risk? People who are awake to

their dreams. What would possess them? Passion. What would propel them forward? Purpose. Who would allow their dreams, passions, and purpose to drive them to boldly climb their Everest, to attain their dream? Yes, it is you, and now is the time to embrace your dream.

We all have the opportunity to live fully and passionately. We were all born with the possibility of doing something distinctly our own, of transforming ourselves into the person we would like to be, of contributing to the world around us or participating more fully in life. Living is often what we make it. Living proactively, living your life inspired by your own calling, creates purpose in your life. Imagine yourself waking up each day secure in the knowledge that on this day you will be engaged with life and aligned with your heart's greatest desires.

Have you limited your vision to being "average"? Are you beginning to recognize that you want to do more in your life? Are you willing to allow the blinders to be peeled away, to live proactively? Are you ready to wake to your true dream and courageously step out of the average into extraordinary?

Surrender and let the debris of unfulfilled dreams, goals, and desires begin to fall away. As you come to this moment in time, reading these words, allow yourself to feel your body, mind, emotions, spirit, and heart waking up. Allow yourself to begin realizing that limitless potential resides within you, waiting to be claimed.

The first step on this journey of awakening to your potential is to take a good look at your current life. Whose dreams, goals, and visions are you living? Are they yours or someone else's? Do you have your own vision of what you want out of life? This part is crucial because you need to focus your time and energy to pursue goals that are the most motivating for you.

My parents wanted me to choose a comfortable life, one they could be proud of. They wanted me to choose a safe career with long-term prospects, a secure income, and a good retirement plan. They both had degrees in teaching and had hoped I would follow in their footsteps. It was also important to them for me to marry earlier rather than later, have a couple of children, and enjoy the country club lifestyle.

I tried for many years to live the life my parents wanted me to live. I continued to try to get their acceptance. I majored in psychology and recreation therapy, although it did not exactly promise high financial rewards in the end. I got degrees and credentials in elementary education and in addition, I received credentials to teach children with special needs. I had various jobs in education that created an illusion of security.

But because I was not in synch with my true passions, I kept veering from this path. Instead of playing it safe I began to explore challenging sports such as adventure racing, which involves multi-day, multi-sport, non-stop racing, often in a four-person format. I also took summer jobs as a Class 3, 4, and 5 whitewater rafting river guide on the American, Kern, and Klamath Rivers. I was exploring my own "boots." I was working towards recognizing the increasingly demanding parts of myself that I had denied in an attempt to please my parents.

So for awhile I decided to fragment my life. I chose

to do a part of what my parents wanted me to do, be in a career that represented security, and the other portion of the time I followed my heart and explored the adventure that was more in alignment with my true self. Examples of this included: bike touring in the United States and overseas, multi-day backpacking trips, multi-day river trips, and competitive endurance sports. Finally, when I was in my late thirties I'd had it with the fragmentation. I became secure enough in myself that I decided to do life my way, to hike fully and freely in my own boots regardless of anyone else's desire for me. I had discovered what should have been obvious, that you can waste a great deal of time trying to do the right thing with someone else's dream for you, but after all the effort, in the end you are the only one left feeling empty.

Every moment in life is a gift. The choice is yours to receive the moment or to reject or deny it. You can let it live or you can suffocate or stuff it.

Chapter One Exercises

Call to Action: Questions That Facilitate Waking
Up to Your Passion

1. What did you love to do as a child? Make a list.

    What did you gravitate to?
    What did you think about, explore, learn about, or
    participate in?

2. Remember your most perfect day to date. Describe
    this in detail.

    What were you doing?
    Who were you with?
    What about the experience was satisfying, fulfill-
    ing, passion driven?

2 | Finding Your Boots

"Define your future by your dreams and not by your memories, by your hopes and not your fears."
—Joe Tye, *Your Dreams Are Too Small*

Now that you have decided to take the plunge and step up to new challenges, you need to figure out how to make changes in your life. Think of this as searching for boots that fit you. This chapter explores what it means to "find your hiking boots," to find your way in what may be uncharted territory. You will also learn to "lace up your boots"; that is, to learn the lessons that are essential for a successful journey.

Keep in mind there are many pieces of climbing gear you will need on this journey, including tools such as affirmations and visualizations to bolster your confidence and overcome your fear. You will also need to find supportive people, like coaches and mentors, who will help you learn the skills and strategies you need to succeed. In the chapters to come I will talk more about these tools.

But first, you need to be standing firmly in your own boots. Although you will find that everyone's boots are different, the process we experience while hiking in them is universal in that we are all moving step-by-step towards our goals.

I remember a powerful learning experience on my third day of climbing during our summit attempt. We started out at seven in the morning from Camp Two, which is at 25,500 feet and moved towards camp three, which is 27,700 feet. This 2,200-foot gain was on steep and dangerous terrain. During this part of the journey we were required to use oxygen for the first time, and we continued to be on fixed line all the way up to camp three. Fixed lines are ropes attached to hardware that the Sherpas pound into the side of the mountain. Each climber clips into the fixed line with an ascender, a piece of hardware that clips into the fixed line, which helps climbers ascend. This is a safety precaution in case someone slips and falls.

When I arrived at the two-man tent that I would be sharing with two of my fellow climbers, I found that the Sherpas had stacked the extra oxygen bottles inside. Because it was a two-man tent to be shared by three people and all of our gear, I decided it would be a good idea to move all the oxygen bottles outside. As I was moving the oxygen, one of the bottles slipped out of my hands. To my horror it actually went careening down the mountain. The Sherpas joined in my total disbelief of what had just happened.

There were three important aspects of this mishap. First, there was a very specific amount of oxygen for each person, and losing one of the bottles could create a shortage that might jeopardize a life. Second, the oxygen bottles are $400 each, so to have one lost on the mountain was a costly error. Three, an oxygen bottle rapidly gains speed at as it bounces down the mountain, and it could easily kill someone on the route. Luckily in this case no one was injured.

As the oxygen bottle was racing down the mountain it had to cross the route where people were climbing up. What could I do? Yell! So I yelled at the top of my lungs to the climbers below, drawing their attention to the out-of-control oxygen bottle. I was hoping and praying that it would not hit anybody. I had an intense sinking feeling during those moments.

This experience was a dangerous and costly error. I had to decide what I was going to do next. I had two options: I could accept what happened and move on, or I could hold on to this event and allow it to take me out of the present moment, which could potentially lead to more errors. To me, there was only one choice—accept what happened, learn from my mistake, forgive, and move on.

One of the teammates got so upset with me that he was yelling, cursing at me, visibly very angry. After I profusely apologized he calmed down. I would not say that he was fine, but he calmed down. However, you could feel the tension for at least a few more hours.

To hold on to the emotions that were directed at me, to continually replay them in my mind would have been a set-up for potential failure. Therefore, I took this opportunity to once again forgive.

I learned a valuable lesson from this experience. I learned to be careful and to remember that everything we do matters. It is imperative that you are careful and pay attention to every step along the way.

There is an important consideration to think about as you explore what it means to be climbing in your own boots. And that is your clarity of purpose. How do you know you have chosen the right dream or goal for yourself? In my experience, if it is the right goal it will involve a combination of your strengths and your passions. I also believe that you will feel the "rightness" physically in the form of excitement, increased energy, possibly some fear, and often a desire to get started on the plan. If I am pursuing something that creates only some of the above responses, or that feels more luke-warm than boiling hot, I know I am most likely not on track.

Chapter Two Exercises

Call to Action: Finding Your Boots

1. Take an internal inventory. When you write down your dream or goal how does it feel? Can you visualize it? Does it create excitement, passion, and desire to move forward? Do you feel possible fear?

2. Commit yourself to what inspires you most. Write down three things you can do every day to move you closer to your goal.

3. When we are in alignment with our goals and dreams, the "law of attraction" tends to appear. What is showing up in your life to support your choice and move you forward? Make a list.

3 | Lacing Your Boots—Know What You Want

"If you know you want it, HAVE IT!"
—Gita Bellin, *Amazing Grace Series*

As I look back on the journey that took me to the top of the world I realize that my childhood fascination and dream to one day climb Mount Everest has guided my accomplishments over the years. The process of working to achieve my goals, at each stage of my life, gave me the physical, mental, and emotional endurance I would need.

I enjoyed outdoor adventure, which led to becoming a white water river guide. Then I moved into adventure racing. Adventure racing is a multi-sport, often multi-day, non-stop race that is typically done in teams of four people. At least one team member must be a person of the opposite sex. The disciplines include sports like hiking, running, mountain biking, rafting, ocean paddling, rappelling, ascending, and river kayaking. Each step along the way I gave myself permission to play, dream bigger, and explore. I challenged myself physically, mentally, and emotionally. I pushed myself to the limits and found with each step forward that my energy expanded giving me more capacity to grow.

Before planning my Mount Everest climb, I had climbed a few mountains in Colorado and Mount Shasta in California, but I hadn't climbed anything higher or harder than Mount Whitney's peak of 14,505 feet in Lone Pine, California. I started working with coaches and mentors to prepare for the Mount Everest ascent. They advised me to step out of my comfort zone and to climb a mountain higher and harder than Mount Whitney. This would give me an indication of what I might face on a Mount Everest expedition. Knowing what I would potentially experience would give me further clarity and wisdom in my final decision about whether or not to proceed.

I learned that when you are clear what your goal is, the next step is to begin to cover the ground that will take you closer. Your next step will undoubtedly look different yet will accomplish the same thing. It will build your confidence, giving you the energy to keep moving forward. It will strengthen your intention which erases any doubt about where you are headed. It will provide you with valuable information related to your progress or need for reevaluation.

I chose to climb Mount Denali in Alaska, which would test my readiness for something bigger and harder. Denali, also known as Mount McKinley, is 20,320 feet; many climbers say that it simulates other peaks in the Himalayas. They claim that its close promimity to the Arctic Circle provides climbers with essential experience of very cold temperatures. People use this mountain as training for climbing bigger, harder mountains because the terrain is challenging and the temperatures can simulate the icy, bitter cold of Mount Everest. Denali can be either horrific or kind depending on the weather and conditions of the day. A person can climb Denali and get a full Mount Everest type experience, tested to the max, or their experience can be fairly benign.

As far as the technical part of climbing there wasn't anything in the United States that comes close to the technical difficulty Denali offers short of heading over to the Himalayas. Denali challenges climbers to face their fears. It challenges their physical strength and fortitude by providing hard fixed-line climbing, exposure to the elements, and steep terrain with variable weather conditions.

Denali is often used as a testing ground for Everest because it has a challenging fixed-line section on the Washburn (normal route), which is called the headwall. It also has a ridge section that is tricky and exposed. This gives climbers a glimpse of what to expect for much of the route on Everest. It was these two features of the Denali climb—the fixed-line and the ridge section—that helped me gain more confidence about meeting the challenges that I knew I would face on Everest.

I knew what I wanted. I wanted to climb Mount Everest. Knowing what I wanted motivated me to plan my route. Planning my route included gathering necessary tools like appropriate coaching, physical preparation, and acquiring the best gear for the journey. I had to take all these baby steps. I continued to hold onto the vision. I trusted the process. I proceeded with clarity.

Look for your own signs that you are on your right

track. What baby steps do you need to take to move you closer to where you want to go? What kinds of things will strengthen your clarity of purpose? What I find invaluable is the process of writing down my goal and then making a plan to accomplish it. This could involve many areas and types of activities. Your goal may have several components that need to be accomplished. Begin the process of writing down your most important goals and considering your plan. We will cover this process in the next few chapters.

I will never forget that day when clarity struck, and I decided that climbing Mount Everest was definitely going to happen. I had met some people who were planning to climb Mount Everest. They invited me to go with them, and I thought that this would be the perfect opportunity for me. Right then I had luminous clarity: "YES. I am doing it. I am going to climb Mount Everest."

I could not contain my excitement and passion. After the early morning meeting, I got in my car and opened my windows. I drove down Mount Shasta Boulevard shouting, "I'm going to climb Mount Everest and I am going to do it as a fund raiser." I was fully alive in undeniable clarity.

With my clarity and commitment everything in my life began to support my forward momentum. My whole body woke up. I felt awake and alive on every level. I was doing it. I was actually going to live my dream. I had no idea how it would happen. However, I knew beyond a shadow of a doubt and with every cell of my body that I was going to do it. Even though it took another year before I actually made it to Mount Everest,

I knew in that moment exactly where I was going. I never gave up. I continued to proceed in forward motion with a crystal clear knowledge that I would climb that mountain.

I have had other experiences just like this in which totally clarity was present. One very vivid experience was related to the online clothing business I started while pregnant with my daughter Avriel. Fit Maternity, the online business that I started, was my response to a need that pregnant women have; it was a way to support women wanting to be active during their pregnancies. I was absolutely alive, motivated, passionate, and scared about the financial commitment. Yet all these same emotions kept me moving forward to create a very successful internet business.

Another experience of clarity of purpose that comes to mind was when I made a decision to become involved in the sport of adventure racing. I can recall exactly how this came about, and how I was feeling when I decided to pursue it. I was watching a television show (very unusual for me) called the "Eco Challenge, Morocco." I was glued to my seat, barely able to contain my excitement as I watched the racers make their way from check point to check point with all kinds of challenges and issues. As soon as the show ended I knew that I wanted to find my way onto a world class team.

This was easier said than done, but with systematic commitment, a few months later I was racing, and a year later I was racing with various world class, sponsored teams. These examples are meant to show you how get in touch with what really speaks to you, keeps you motivated, and feels worthwhile in every cell of your body.

With clarity you can move forward. You can jump in with both feet and commit to your journey. Each step will have purpose. You will want to shout it out to the world, "I am doing it." You know where you are going beyond a shadow of a doubt. The power of "YES, I am doing it" propels you. Finding clarity can take some work. Sometimes just sitting with the possibilities is a way to feel clarity. The more you are personally aligned with your goals and priorities, the more support seems to show up. One way I can gauge the veracity of my choices is to reflect on whether I standing alone with no momentum or whether events and opportunities are beginning to fall into place in a way that supports my goal. You can use this gauge too.

Chapter Three Exercises

Call to Action: Dream Big Dreams

1. Imagine that you have found a magic lamp with a genie who will grant you ANY three wishes. On a separate piece of paper, list your wishes.

2. Write down what makes you happiest and gives you the most purpose for your life.

3. What you think about and visualize determines your behavior and your results. What do you think and talk about most of the time?

4 | Choosing Wisely

"You can't just sit there and wait for people to give you that golden dream, you've got to get out there and make it happen yourself."
—Diana Ross, *Sunshine Book of Quotes*

I have been asked, "How do I know what to go for in my life?"

My response is, "Does the thought of your dream create a feeling of excitement and purpose? Is it a bit daunting? Does it scare you? Is it something you have thought of over the years? Is it constantly on your mind? Do you have a passion for it? If you didn't go for it, how would you feel?"

I believe the big dream to go for is the one you feel in your whole body. There will be passion for it that leads to a burning desire. There will be nothing lukewarm about it. I have discovered that if I pursued goals that did not bring out this kind of excitement there ultimately would be a lack of commitment and desire to continue on the path. The right dream creates the power and passion to go beyond all obstacles. It drives you to succeed. You will know when you have hit on it, because even when things are hard, tedious, and exhausting you will feel that it is still worth it to keep moving forward.

When I decided to climb Everest I was very passionate about the dream. I had no idea what it would really be like, and I can tell you that without this initial passion and desire I would not have lasted through the ordeal. I can give you a few examples of how glamorous and fun-filled this journey was.

Once I got to Advanced Base Camp (ABC) things really changed. A typical morning would begin with temperatures below zero. I would awaken, usually very tired, after a night of little sleep, because we were all experiencing sleep apnea, to a tent filled with ice crystals from our frozen breath. I would try to get dressed without getting covered in the crystals by accidentally brushing against them. Next was the process of brushing teeth with often mostly frozen water, because even though I slept with my water bottles to avoid this they often froze. After that was the ever-pleasant task of putting on mostly frozen boots (even though we slept with those in the tent as well). This could take up to fifteen minutes of cramming my feet into the boots, tugging, and pulling to get them on, freezing my fingers in the process, and all the while hoping I could hold off on going to the bathroom until the boots were actually on my feet. This was no easy undertaking. Last was the mad dash to the bathroom bucket which is a story all unto itself. The trick was not to go so fast that you became hypoxic but not so slow that you were embarrassed later. This was all so much fun. And it was just the start of the day. When I was actually climbing, things were much more difficult in all areas. It became a mental game of fortitude to stay the course for six weeks in order to be ready for a summit attempt.

It is wise to carefully choose which mountain you will climb. I had climbed many mountains and could have chosen a mountain harder than Mount Everest. But I chose *this* mountain, the top of the world. Harder mountains are not necessarily the best mountains to climb. In choosing wisely you will summit the mountain that is right for you. It may not be the hardest one; however, it will be the perfect one for you.

During my climb, I gave myself permission to stop moving forward and return to Base Camp if at any point something didn't feel right. I also gave myself permission to take five more steps...ten more steps... continue on for one more minute...five more minutes. After moving forward I would review the situation again. If I still felt that I needed to turn back, fine. It was that five more steps that took me all the way to the summit of Mount Everest.

As you set goals and achieve them, your excitement will be fueled. Yes, you will also experience challenges along the way. Be diligent. Give yourself permission to keep going another five steps even when it feels too difficult. Soon the energy of achieved goals will take on a life of its own like a snowball rolling down a mountain gathering more snow and tremendous momentum. This momentum will attract the support and assistance you need to actualize your goal. You will find that people, events, and circumstances will continue to show up to assist you on your journey. Your job is to stay focused.

A friend and mentor, Hooman Aprin, told me a wonderful story related to this very concept. He was on the team of Sherpas that fix the line that all the other climbers use to safely ascend to the summit. The Sherpas that take on this job are exposed to tremendous risk and often horrific weather conditions. None of the climbers that have paid to climb will move forward until this task is completed. Hooman said that as he was climbing ever higher, fixing the line and putting in protection, his whole focus was on staying safe, getting the line safely in place, and moving forward one step at a time. He said that when he reached the top of Everest he was very surprised; he had been so intent on the task at hand that he had not realized the team of Sherpas that was managing the fixed line was closing the gap to the summit. His advice to me, which I bring to you, was, "Be calm, focused, and relentless on your climb."

It is important to choose wisely. When the storms hit, you want to know that your foundation is solid and that you have the confidence to weather all kinds of adversity and still succeed. Some ideas around choosing wisely include: Does your choice feel exciting, scary, motivating, and compelling? Are you experiencing forward flow around your choice or constant road blocks and adversity?

I have found that when I have made the right choice, moving forward may not be easy, but there is a certain amount of ease that has always emerged when my choice is in alignment with my passions, talents, and strengths. I also believe that when we make the right choices we feel it in our entire being. That was certainly what happened for me when I became committed to my goal. Pay close attention to your body and mind when you think about the goal you have chosen. Do you feel it not only mentally but physically as well?

I have a very strong memory of the day I made the commitment to climb Mount Everest. It was early in the winter of 2004. I had just had a conversation with a climber who had climbed Mount Everest from the South Route. He had also attempted to climb the North Col Route, the route I wanted to climb. Through our conversation I began to get a much clearer picture of what I was considering. This created a feeling of tremendous excitement as well as heart-stopping fear.

I remembered thinking, "Can I consider taking on something that I know could kill me?" In the same breath what I felt was, "I so much want to explore this huge dream and turn it into a reality."

I experienced a tremendous surge of energy coursing through my body. I was shouting within the silence of my own being from the depths of my heart, "I am climbing Mount Everest! I am climbing Mount Everest!" I could feel it. I knew in this moment I was committed. Everything within me said "Yes." I had made my decision. I would not turn back. I felt simultaneously nervous and scared. I also felt courageous and ready to move forward. I believe that when we are in alignment with our goal we may experience self-doubt, discouragement, or despair, but we will still see the value in continuing on.

I had an experience on summit day that reflects this same principle. My Sherpa, Nema Cheri, was leading the way as we approached the summit traverse. This part of the climb came after what I thought were all the hard sections. Was I in for a surprise. The traverse is on a section of the route that consists of icy slabs of rock and scree, which is loose rock that tends to move. This section of the route is also referred to as off camber because you are not going up or down but sideways, which is very difficult since you have to walk in big boots over loose, icy rock with little protection.

The rope was poorly fixed here, lying on the snow. There was no protection for my Sherpa. He had no object to anchor himself to so he could belay or assist me using the rope. My level of anxiety increased further as I followed after Nema on this section, because I was horrified to see at least four bodies lying on the mountain below this part of the route. Obviously climbers before me over the years and even recently had fallen to their deaths here. This section had to be navigated in order to reach the last stretch to the summit. I do remember thinking that perhaps I was in over my head, but retreating was going to be very perilous once I began moving forward.

With all the courage I could muster, I began the treacherous walk on the traverse towards the part of the route which continued to ascend. As you begin the process of pursuing your dream, you will encounter times when it will take all you have to move forward. What I recommend doing at that point is to give yourself permission to take a deep breath and focus on the present moment, situation, or challenge. Figure out your plan and move forward even if it is only a baby step a day.

In closing this chapter, I share the personal account

of a woman who wanted to change the direction of her life; I coached her on the path to achieving her dream using the same steps that I outline for you in this book. Take heart from her words; her story can be your own.

In 2001 I contacted Laurie because of my longing to get into better shape. I had been more athletic in the past and a few pounds lighter but at that time I was stuck in a less than desirable fitness slump! I also knew something about myself—the healthier and fitter I am, the stronger I feel both physically and emotionally. It was time to make a difference and I was ready for help.

When I had my first conversation with Laurie she assessed my current and potential physical shape and said to my surprise, "How about setting the goal to climb Mt. Shasta?" I was astonished and excited immediately.

"Could I really do that?" I asked myself, full of doubt.

Laurie, as if reading my mind, responded, "Sometimes I think it is a good idea to have a goal—something to reach for. And I know, Joy, you can climb Mt. Shasta with a bit of consistent training over the next months."

Over that late winter and early spring I worked with Laurie to develop, strategize, and finally achieve my goal of summiting Mt. Shasta. Her guidance and clear direction helped me to stick with daily, weekly, and monthly milestones that brought me closer to what I wanted, the summit AND more importantly a sense of self-worth, confidence, and power that physical exercise can bring women.

Laurie's process is full of self-reflection, inspiration, reality, and new insights into dreaming big and following through each step of the way. In my experience with Laurie I exceeded my initial expectations and actually surprised myself with how far I could go to be an athletic woman again!

I have also attended her workshop, and as a business consultant and trainer myself, I appreciated how carefully Laurie covered material making sure all participants were feeling the profound teachings embedded in going for our highest potential. Laurie shares from experience and therefore a transfer of energy offers participants ultimate success in many areas of life. Her understanding of values and priorities helps people do what is right for them and pursue their truest dreams.

I am continually grateful for her message, compassion, and example of a woman who can be committed to what is right for her!

Joy von Skepsgardh, LivingVisionsNow.com

Chapter Four Exercises

Call to Action: Choosing Wisely and Finding the Courage to Move Forward

1. How would you feel if you accomplished your big dream/goal today?

2. What are the major fears that hold you back from pursuing your dreams/goals?

3. List the things that make you happiest and give you the most purpose in your life.

5 | The Ever Important "Why?"

"There is one quality which one must possess to win, and that is definiteness of purpose, the knowledge of what one wants, and a burning desire to possess it."
—Napoleon Hill, *The Law of Success*

Frequently I have been asked why I decided to climb Everest when the ratio of climbers who summit to climbers who die on Mount Everest was seven to one in 2003. In other words, for every seven climbers that reach the summit, one person died. If I had known this statistic before I made my commitment, I don't know if I would have attempted the journey. What I did know was that I had many inner reasons for attempting this climb. I relied on my "whys" often when things got tough.

As a young woman of sixteen, I had an intense interest in climbing Mount Everest. I was attracted to climbing, which led to the dream of Mount Everest, which, in turn, captured my mind and heart. I read everything I could about this mountain (and still do). I was twenty-six before the first woman made the summit of Mount Everest. Knowing that one woman had climbed all the way to the summit gave me the courage to imagine that I could be one of the few women to view life from the top of the world. Holding this vision became one of my "whys."

To engage in a challenging climbing expedition such as Mount Everest, you must be prepared physically, mentally, and emotionally. Throughout my childhood, teen years, and into adulthood I excelled in competitive endurance sports. Long-distance running, cycling, and competitive mountain-bike racing taught me a lot about endurance. I believe that during my life I took on harder and harder challenges in order to test myself. I always seemed to excel if I engaged in more difficult endeavors. These activities prepared me for the rigors that high altitude mountaineering demand.

When I finally retired from adventure racing at the age of forty-three in 2004, I thought I was done with competition; however, I felt that I still had not challenged myself fully. It was at this point that opportunities to climb Mount Everest began to show up in my life. Why climb Mount Everest? My "why" was to challenge myself to achieve my full potential. To take this motivation a step further, I also felt it was incredibly valuable to provide a model to show my daughter and other women and girls that anything is possible if you're willing to take all the steps, do all the hard work, and get all your tools and supports in place.

As a woman who has not followed more traditional female roles, and as a mother who is committed to allowing her daughter to hike in her own boots, I felt that I had an opportunity to "walk my talk," as the saying goes. This created an additional purpose for my goal. I wanted my daughter to see that having the necessary

tools and strategies in place establishes a greater possibility for success.

Why? What would possess you to want to climb a
particular metaphoric mountain? What would make
you choose that mountain? Why would you risk your
old life, old beliefs, and comfort to climb anything?

The "why" of your journey, the reason for choosing a
specific goal, is essential to your success. If your "why"
is weak, it becomes a weak link in the climbing rope,
and since your "climbing rope" is a lifeline, you need it
to be strong. When adversity shows up you will want a
strong "why" to hold on to.

A solid "why" can get you to your summit and back
down the mountain. Your "why" will support your commitment, assist you in choosing wisely, give you courage to keep moving forward, bolster your confidence,
aid your flexibility, and anchor your personal pledge.
Finding your "why" is the bottom line to creating a successful journey.

You will find yourself relying on this "why" to support you like a rope on your climb. When you slip it
will be there for you to grab on to. It will catch you if
you stumble and fall. When the storms hit, your "why"
becomes your anchor and protection. It is a foundation
piece of your climbing gear.

Know your "why" intimately, deeply, vividly, and with
every cell of your body. Write it out several times. Let
it shift, morph, and change until it speaks to the very
core of your body, mind, emotions, and being. Work
with it until you have a solid response that says, "Yes,

this is why!"

Come to know your "why" so intimately that it is clamped onto your hiking boots like the crampons, the spikes that hold you firmly on the path. Let your "why" give you the confidence to take every step all the way to the top of the world with steadfast assurance. Your "why" gives you the confidence to know that this journey was meant for you and you were meant for this journey.

My experience is that in order to stay the course you must get to the bottom reason of why you chose the goal that you did. Rarely have I seen anyone finding that financial gain was enough of a reason. The "Call to Action" exercises at the end of these chapters that encourage you to sit with your dream and write it down will help you deepen your exploration. In addition, being willing to change your goal if it is not powerful enough can make a big difference in your ability to hang on when the storm is ferocious.

One of the strategies that I have found particularly helpful in pursuing my goal when the going gets tough is dedicating my goal to someone or something other than myself. This act of reaching beyond oneself to a higher cause creates a universal feeling of contribution, which can be more powerful than just personal desire. When it becomes difficult to meet a challenge or sometimes even a struggle, you can reflect on who or what you have dedicated your big goal to. Any goal reaches deeper meaning, fulfillment, and satisfaction when it is dedicated to a higher purpose, something greater than oneself. This dedication or association to something larger gives you the extra incentive to follow through in all kinds of weather.

I was fortunate to know what my dream was, then set goals, and finally take the necessary actions to accomplish them. I consider it a gift that I had the opportunity to climb, summit, and make it back down from Mount Everest safely. This was certainly a turning point for me. I knew that I could make this dream serve a greater purpose. There was a part of me that felt an immense need, a desire, and an obligation to step outside of my comfort zone and reach into the larger community as a catalyst for others to experience change in their lives. Should you choose to dedicate your goal to someone or something make sure it is powerful and motivating for you.

I dedicated my Mount Everest climb, in spirit and resources, to Kirwin International Relief Foundation. Known as KIRF INDIA Foundation, this is a non-profit organization that provides education and medical assistance to the poor children in Bodhgaya, India. I chose to raise money during my pre-Everest climb and also did fund raisers for this organization after I returned. With many successful pre- and post-climb events that included slide and media shows, I was able to raise more than ten thousand dollars for this organization.

Diane Kirwin and KIRF INDIA are inspirations to me. The awareness that I was supporting Diane's work in India gave me an extra pound of passion to successfully complete my climb. I was not only climbing for myself; I was climbing for the children. Friends of mine created a prayer flag representing KIRF INDIA for me to take on the expedition. It inspired me to keep going. It was a constant reminder that my climb was important to someone other than myself. It reminded me that every step on the path was serving a higher purpose.

Along with this commitment came the amazing support of a group of women in the community that worked with me to promote, organize, and facilitate all the fund raising events we had. This was a huge, unexpected gift. These women had nothing to gain except the knowledge that they were helping me to accomplish my goal, and they were catalysts in making a difference for KIRF. A gift that came from this was continued support from the group while I was climbing. I recall one situation in particular when I emailed a couple of the women expressing my doubt about continuing on with the summit attempt.

My friend Lauren replied, "Go for it. We are here for you!" She later told me how torn she was about encouraging me in the event that something bad might happen. It was these kinds of events that kept me focused on the greater sense of purpose.

As you look at your goals, ask yourself, "What higher purpose am I aligned with?" Turning personal accomplishment into a greater purpose will expand your momentum and drive. The synergy of working in alignment with something worthwhile not only adds personal satisfaction; it develops extra power to fuel your potential.

When you dream big for a cause, you will attract others to take part in your dream. Linking your dream to solving a common problem will accelerate your progress on the path. Living with purpose and meaning is a key to great successes. When you recognize that your endeavors are a gift to the world and an example of human greatness, you offer more than a personal accomplishment. You offer your strengths as a demonstration of what every human being can become. This gives you more energy to stay focused throughout the process or event. Your accomplishments become an offering to the world, not just a personal possession.

It has been my experience that finding the greater purpose associated with your big dream or goal will keep you more motivated when things get rough. Of course, what you do may benefit you greatly, but can it make a difference for others? When you can answer this question with a solid "Yes" you are much less likely to get derailed.

Chapter Five Exercises

Call to Action: Answering the Very Important "Why?" and Finding the Higher Purpose

1. Begin by making a list of sentences that start with the phrase "I want to accomplish the goal because...." Keep writing new sentences as fast as you can for five minutes.

2. Examine your list. Pick out the top three statements that feel true and most important.

3. Write, rewrite, and work those three statements until they feel as natural to say as your name and as familiar as your favorite clothing. This is your "why." Speak it, wear it, possess it, and be possessed by it. Make yourself inseparable from it, and it from you.

4. Can you think of a way your dream/goal can help someone or something?

5. If it involves an organization make a list of several organizations that you believe in and would like to support.

6. How can you serve a higher purpose and assist this organization or other individuals through the achievements of your goals?

Part II

Going to the Next Level

In Part Two you will explore more items to add to your pack. Confidence is one component to your success that you can build up gradually. By doing the thing that stretches your comfort zone you learn that you can do it!

As you gain confidence, trusting your intuition and remaining flexible as you continue forward will be necessary. This requires skills related to listening; you need to notice what is supporting your goal, and you need to be willing to make route corrections as you climb your mountain.

Next, making a commitment to yourself will add fuel and momentum to your journey. A personal pledge and someone to be accountable to are tools that can greatly assist this process. And finally, you need an honest evaluation of your past experience and accomplishments and where you are currently. This is crucial. In order to make a plan and take steps to move you closer to your vision, you have to know where you are starting.

6 | Confidence, Your Ally

"Go confidently in the direction of your dreams! Live the life you've imagined."
—Henry David Thoreau, *Sunshine Book of Quotes*

Without confidence, mountains are never climbed, goals are not realized, dreams go unfulfilled, and life is lived in a shrouded comfort zone.

Confidence is a skill that must well up from inside of you. You must come face to face with confidence, shake its hand, and agree to make it your constant companion and friend. As you climb your mountain you will face many situations where your confidence will be needed to pull you through the challenging times. Draw on your inner awareness that you are on your right path, stand tall, and keep moving forward. This approach assisted me on my journey upwards. It will do the same for you.

It was approximately eleven at night when we began our climb to the summit of Everest. The only lights visible were the climbers' headlamps and the stars in the midnight heavens above. I was the first in my group to journey toward the summit with my Sherpa, Nema. A short time into the climb, the light in my headlamp went out. This could have shaken my confidence; however, I chose to go forward relying on Nema's headlamp to light the way for both of us.

Nema and I arrived at the Second Step which is said to be the hardest part of the climb. The Second Step is a steep rock wall section that is ninety feet high. To gain the upper ridge, climbers must move over this rock face via ledges, hand holds, and fixed line. At the top section of the Second Step there is a thirty-foot ladder that is secured against a vertical cliff. Climbers must negotiate this ladder with crampons on their boots, bulky down suits, oxygen masks, and oxygen bottles, all of which make it impossible for the climbers to see their feet. This attire is very cumbersome and makes a dangerous part of the journey even more treacherous. The ladder leads to a very small rock ledge that is no more than two feet in diameter. Once on this small platform, climbers must stand on the ledge, navigate piles of old ropes left from years of climbing expeditions, and then pull themselves up and around the corner of a vertical face of rock. A lot of people have died on this section either by falling off the ledge or entangling themselves in the ropes while ascending or descending and freezing to death.

As Nema and I faced the Second Step we needed to make a decision to either wait for the rest of our group to arrive or continue to climb. We decided to wait. This decision brought its own challenges. We were not moving and it was very cold. In these temperatures it is easy for the body to go into hyperthermia and climbers can quickly freeze to death. Still, we waited until we saw the rest of our group coming before we continued to climb.

Nema and I started up the section above the ladder, which involved free climbing on the rock face until we reached the ladder. Nema started up the ladder first, climbed it with no problem, and went up and over the vertical cliff and disappeared. He was gone and so was the light from his headlamp. It was about five thirty in the morning by this time, so there was barely any light. It was up to me to get myself up the last rungs of the ladder and gain the ridge without getting tangled up in the rope.

Nema had been in my visual sight the whole climb until now. This was different. I had no idea that I would face this kind of challenge. I gained the rock ledge and in an attempt to clear the coiled ropes one of my worst fears came true; my feet got tangled up in the ropes and I could not move. I knew where I was supposed to go but I couldn't physically move. I knew if I took one missstep at this point it was a 10,000-foot drop off the side of the mountain. I was frozen with fear.

I couldn't bend over to untangle the ropes from my feet. I could feel panic throughout my whole body almost to the point of hyperventilation. Fear and panic create a shallow rapid breath that uses up a lot of oxygen. I knew this and did my best to control my breathing. I realized I was stuck on the ledge. There was absolutely nothing I could do except wait. Finally, the next person climbing up the ladder behind me realized that I was tangled in the ropes. To my relief and gratitude he gently pulled the ropes away from my crampons. I was finally free to move. I was able to gain the vertical cliff and continue the climb.

During those moments on the ledge I thought, "I don't know about this. I don't know if I am meant to summit. This whole situation seems awfully hit-and-miss. Maybe I am in over my head. Maybe I should go down." However, once I got untangled from the ropes and got to the top where Nema was waiting, my thoughts took a different direction and I thought, "OK. I got through that situation. I can do this. I can go forward." My confidence had been shaken but not lost.

The experiences on this expedition reminded me of an Indiana Jones movie. Just when things seemed to be going smoothly, fifty tarantulas drop from the ceiling of the cave, or a stone comes rolling down the corridor, or the next challenge suddenly pops up. Climbing Mount Everest was a challenge that required me to stay present and alert. It was an exercise in doing what was needed in the moment, letting go of what happened, focusing, and moving forward one step at a time. I challenge you to stay focused and single minded on your journey.

Climbing up the mountain is considered optional. You may have the opportunity to turn around and go back down. Coming down the mountain, on the other hand, is mandatory. Descending is a different experience. You are no longer checking in to see if it is safe or not, you just keep going, regardless, getting to safety as soon as you can. There is no other option.

You must trust yourself to make the right decisions. Allow yourself to have the unshakable confidence in your body, mind, emotions, and intuition. This will assure that the goal you have chosen is just right for you.

Those who climb with you will have confidence in you, and you will have confidence in them.

How do you gain confidence? What kinds of things can you build into your plan that will strengthen your confidence?

Mount Everest was not the first mountain I had climbed. When I made my personal declaration, I knew that Mount Everest was possible for me. Without having the fitness and pain management skills that I had developed through climbing and adventure racing, I would have never attempted to climb this particular mountain. Acquiring skills that serve your goals will give you the confidence you need to summit your mountain of choice.

To build my confidence, every morning for three months prior to the climb, I would light a candle and visualize what it would be like to climb on the last day. I saw and felt myself successfully climbing the Second Step and making it all the way to the summit. I imagined what it would be like to stand on Mount Everest's peak, viewing the Himalayan mountain range around me. I felt myself at the end of the journey safe and sound at Base Camp celebrating the success of the climb. I imagined what it would be like to come home and see my daughter and hold her in my arms again. I believe that this practice gave me the confidence to gain the Second Step, reach the summit, and make it down the mountain safely.

I also had a few affirmations that I repeated at different times during the day. My self-coaching phrases were:

- Get in, get up, and get out.

- There are no shortcuts.

- What would you do if you knew you absolutely could not fail?

These statements were alive within me throughout my whole journey. They gave me the confidence to keep going.

Another experience that required confidence, building skills was the birth process of my daughter. I had decided that I was not going to have any pain medication and as little intervention as possible. Boy, how naive I was! To gain confidence in an arena that I knew nothing about, I went to birthing classes, read books, designed a birth plan and gave it to the hospital; spoke with my doctor and the staff about my wishes. In addition, I pulled in a birth coach, who was a very good friend and nurse, to help me learn, explore, and be familiar with what might come up during labor. I also had a very supportive spouse who agreed to help me during labor with an intervention should I need it.

The birth of my daughter was one of the most painful and physically demanding things I have ever done. Without the confidence I had gained beforehand, there is no doubt in my mind I would not have been able to stick to my plan. The time that I spent developing confidence in an area that was completely foreign to me came to my rescue.

Confidence is an essential part of what I call, metaphorically, "your climbing gear." Confidence will support you through your entire journey when you make it your constant companion and friend.

My experience related to gaining confidence is that by doing something new and making it through the experience, or by doing something that scares you and doing it anyway, you transform your perception of what is possible. Anytime I have been up against either of these scenarios I know that the more often I take on the situation that I am avoiding, or that scares me, the easier the challenge will be next time. This gives me additional confidence to do it again, with more ease, less fear, and more assurance. I encourage you to look at those things that could be affecting your confidence either because you don't want to do them or because they create fear. Think of how you can explore these areas and turn them into confidence builders rather than confidence blockers.

Chapter Six Exercises

Call to Action: Confidence, Your Ally

1. What about your big dream or goal is scary for you? What could you do to begin the process of moving past your fears? Write down at least three action steps.

2. Preparedness is the enemy of fear. Think about a time in your life when you had a big challenge to face. How did you prepare for it, what strategies worked for you?

7 | Flexibility— Keeping Your Options Open

"I can't change the direction of the wind, but I can adjust my sails to always reach my destination."
—Jimmy Dean, *The Sunshine Book of Quotes*

Giving yourself permission to stay flexible throughout your journey is essential. When there is flexibility in your direction, much can be accomplished. Your big goals will happen with more ease, rightness, and purpose. Flexibility will be a valuable part of your climbing gear.

In the world of mountaineering I am constantly reminded of just how important this can be. While training for Everest, I headed up to Alaska to climb Denali as a training climb. As this was my first big, hard mountain I admit that I was on a mission, no one or no thing was going to prevent me from getting to the top. I had a lot to learn about flexibility.

I will never forget the day our team got to high camp at about 18,000 feet. I was so excited and eager to prepare for what I assumed would be the summit attempt the next day. In my inexperience I was not in touch with how tired the climb to high camp had been, nor was I experienced in the weather patterns on this mountain. I remember walking over to the guides' tent intending to find out what I needed to do to be ready in the morning. I could tell by their response that I might have to take a step back. The clear decision was that our team needed a rest day the next day and it was likely the wind would be too strong anyway. To say I was disappointed was an understatement, yet true to their words, the next day proved to be very windy.

In the end, having an extra day to rest and regroup made the difference between making the summit or not. I am convinced of this given how ultimately tired I was when our team did give it a go (in fairly friendly conditions). I remember stumbling back into camp after our thirteen-hour day barely able to make it to my tent. Parts of my Everest project were similar in nature. Sometimes I had to stop pushing and be open to what was being presented. You too will find that when you feel yourself pushing too hard you may want to reconsider. Maybe all you have to do is take a different approach or a step back and the solution or support will appear.

An example of this need to reconsider happened to me well before I even got to Nepal. In 2004, my quest was to find a safe and reliable outfitter. I talked to contacts that had either guided or had gone with outfitters on expeditions. I was given names of outfitters who were respected. I narrowed down my choices and decided to go with an outfitter that a friend of mine had gone with two years previously. The company he had used was in Russia. I made three attempts to wire my deposit to this company and they never received it.

During this frustrating experience of trying to wire money to Russia, I began to research other companies. There was a company in Nepal that actually became more appealing. I finally gave up on my efforts to wire the deposit to Russia. I decided to go with the company in Nepal. The first time I wired this company the transaction completed easily. When the wire transaction went smoothly, I knew in my gut that I had made the right decision.

I could not have known at the time how important the change in outfitters would be. As it turned out, the Nepal outfitter with which I climbed the North Col Route was the only group to have zero fatalities and no frostbite during all summit attempts on this route. The Russian outfitter I had considered had at least one fatality and numerous cases of frostbite.

I was grateful for my ability to stay flexible from the beginning. I persisted in the original wire and also paused to listen to the voice inside that said, "This is not going smoothly. Is there a better choice?" By being flexible and honoring the step back for reflection and integration, I changed my direction and had a safe and successful summit experience.

Stay flexible. When you feel it's right to make a shift, then shift without hesitation. If you stay alert and continue to make the course changes, knowing and trusting at all times that everything is working in concert with you, success will be yours.

Chapter Seven Exercises

Call to Action: Staying Flexible

1. Write down three times in your life when you chose
    to stay flexible. How did staying flexible serve in a
    positive outcome?

2. Remember three times in your life where you chose
    to stay rigid about the path you were taking. How
    did staying rigid affect the outcome of your desired
    results?

8 | Commit to Yourself

"Then the time came when the risk it took to remain tight in a bud was more painful than the risk it took to blossom."

—Anais Nin, *Goodreads.com*

I will never forget the events that took place between May 19 and 21, 2006. About half of our group had decided to take the first weather window and give the summit a go, which was against the advice of our expedition advisor. We had all come down to Base Camp a few days before this to recover from fourteen days at Advanced Base Camp (ABC). We had only been at Base Camp two days when the first weather window opened up. It was hard for me to watch a group from our expedition leave Base Camp and head up the mountain, but I knew that my body was still recovering from illness and fatigue associated with two weeks at Advanced Base Camp, which was at 21,000 feet. A few days later, after our short recovery time at the lower Base Camp, the rest of us headed back up to ABC to wait for the next weather window, which we trusted would show up soon.

During this time many tragic events took place on the mountain. The number of frostbitten and the number of fatalities began increasing. It was during this period that one of many emergency radio calls came in. The first one was related to a French man who had fallen to his death. This was unconfirmed as no one who had seen the man fall had actually returned to ABC yet. Not long after this call, his wife who had also been climbing but had been turned back at Camp Three came to our tent. She was wondering if we had received any news. She was desperate to know what was going on. On Everest it is not appropriate to report fatalities until they are confirmed. We could not give her any information.

Not long after this, the story was verified and she was completely at a loss as to what to do. I helped her with phone calls and offered to help her pack up her things and her husband's things. It was brutally hard to see and feel her grief and pain. It was also difficult to consider the journey I was about to embark on. I remember emailing a few trusted friends expressing my concern, doubt, and fear. Their support and encouragement took me back to that place of commitment to myself. It brought up all the hard work I had done to date. For me, this meant being in the position of a summit attempt; it ultimately confirmed my goal of giving this last phase of the climb a chance.

People often ask me what I went through personally in order to come to a decision to climb Mount Everest. What it took for me was:

First the decision to climb Mount Everest and attempt to summit.

Then the excitement and enthusiasm that allowed

my passion to burn into a heartfelt commitment to my-self. The "I" became very important. With the commit-ment to myself I realized that time is one of the illusive things that can slip away almost without noticing.

I began to guard my time and channel my energy in the direction of my goal. It had to become the most important focus. This is a key component for anyone committed to their big dream/goal. Give attention to your intention. Keep yourself focused on the prize and steer clear of distractions.

The process of committing to climb Mount Everest, knowing that there were elements of the journey that would be out of my hands, took about six months. The process of committing to the journey and believing that I was capable of accomplishing this goal took a year.

The opportunity to climb Mount Everest was first presented to me through an acquaintance who wanted to do the climb with a group of people he knew. I heard about his plans and began dialoguing with him in the spring of 2004. Six months later, in September of 2004, I made a commitment to the climb by sending a deposit of five hundred dollars to secure my spot.

I did have reservations throughout this entire pro-cess. The group going was very budget-minded. They were hiring very little Sherpa support, buying minimal oxygen, and the outfitter provided nominal medical support. No one in the group had any experience on Mount Everest.

After talking to my coaches and mentors at length, I realized that this group was not the one for me to travel with. At the end of October 2004, I canceled my reservation. This in no way shifted my goal. I knew I was going to climb Mount Everest. No portion of my dream, passion, or desire faded. I trusted the shift in course, knowing that the opportunity that was more of a match for me would come along. Safety was very important to me. So I began a new search for a situation that I could align with.

As you move forward with your goal you may run into situations that feel close but are not quite right. It is so easy to ignore your inner wisdom and to make decisions that ultimately don't support your direction. Listen to this self-knowledge, and give yourself permission to change your mind if that is what it takes.

I do remember feeling very discouraged for about a month as I regrouped and began my quest for an outfitting service that met my criteria. I also knew I wanted to raise money for a non-profit organization, utilizing the climb to benefit a cause that I believed in. This delay gave me the opportunity to find a non-profit organization to work with. It also gave me more time to get myself physically and mentally ready for all the unknowns I would be facing. Putting all these things into place helped me combat feeling discouraged and gave me passion, energy, and the desire to keep moving forward.

Once I had this momentum in place, I experienced far fewer red flags. In fact, I think adversity is designed to test our commitment to our goals. The more challenges we experience and are willing to move through, the more solid our commitment becomes.

With this in mind you can measure your level of commitment to yourself. Are you willing to move through adversity? Are you willing to acquire the tools, skills, and support you will need in order to accomplish your big dream or goal? Remember, we never accomplish big things on our own. They are the result of support, cooperation, shared vision, and insight. Being able to honestly answer these questions for yourself is a step in the direction of a solid commitment to the path you are choosing to follow.

Part of making a commitment to yourself could involve a personal pledge. What is a personal pledge and why is it an important consideration for anyone with a big dream or goal? Here's how the dictionary *Words in Definition* defines "personal pledge": "(n.) A promise or agreement by which one binds one's self to do, or to refrain from doing, something; especially, a solemn promise in writing; as, to sign the pledge."

In sum, a personal pledge is an important part of the balance and stability that leads to success. A pledge is an agreement that you make with yourself. It is an agreement that you keep and that keeps you on track. Making a pledge keeps the ego in check and allows you to expand more fully into your accomplishments.

During my training and climbing of Mount Everest I maintained the following personal pledges:

- I pledge to turn around the first time I sense any life-threatening danger that I have control over, including threatening weather, my ability to handle the difficulties of the route, and my ability to physically handle the altitude.

- I pledge to make sure my daughter feels safe and understands the reasons that I am climbing Mount Everest and why I will be gone for two months in order to do so.

- I pledge to give this goal one hundred percent, and if I choose not to summit it does not mean I failed.

By making these pledges my mind and ego could be satisfied and feel safe throughout the climb. The ego knew that if it got to be too much, too hard, or not safe, I would turn around and go back down the mountain. Quieting the ego and mind will assist you in staying present to the moment. By staying present to the moment all appropriate decisions and steps can be made to insure a successful journey.

One experience that is vivid to me and reflects the reason that having a pledge can be valuable had to do with our summit team and our wait for a predicted second weather window. During the time that the first weather window had come and gone, seven fatalities and over a dozen cases of frostbite occurred. My confidence began to waver. As I sat waiting for our group's turn, I started to doubt the whole reason I had made it this far to begin with.

I remember at one point going to our expedition advisor with my doubts. His response was, "You've come this far. I can't advise you to continue but I can strongly recommend it." At the same time, the second advisor supporting our team, owner of the outfitting service and advisor for another team, was busy trying to get his group off the mountain since they had gone during the first window of opportunity to summit. His advice made a huge impression on me as well. I knew he was making arrangements for his group to head back to Katmandu as soon as possible, and I had a fleeting thought that I could join them. When I asked about the possibility he said, "You need to give this mountain a try." He was well aware of the commitment I had made with myself, as he was the one who had interviewed me for a spot with his outfitting company. As I sat with both of these men's counsel it became easier for me to let go of my fear and move forward with my commitment to myself which was "show up and climb."

There will be highs and lows in the adventure you are on. A personal pledge allows passion and action to be balanced in a way that keeps passion alive and well through all kinds of weather and adversity. My experience, which I send your way, is to be prepared for the hard times that will arise. Continually renew your commitment to yourself either with affirmations, journal writing, a conversation with a trusted friend, or a session with a coach or mentor. The commitment is to yourself, and having people you trust supporting in this can be valuable

Chapter Eight Exercises

Call to Action: Commit to Yourself

1. What tools, supports, skills, or knowledge would help you commit more fully to your dream/goal and ultimately to yourself?

2. Find at least one person (creating a team is even better) who you can trust and be accountable to in regards to your commitment to yourself. Make a plan that involves contact related to your dream/goal and supports your progress.

Call to Action: Personal Pledge

1. Write down three intentions that reflect your values. Be clear and specific and write the intentions in present time. Example: My intention is to spend more time with my daughter by creating a special time for the two of us at least once a week by October 2010.

2. Write down a personal pledge for each intention.

3. Review what you have written. How does each statement and pledge feel? Do they feel true? Do they feel doable? The time to begin implementing these intentions and pledges is today!

9 | Evaluating Where You Are

"Do what you can, with what you have and where you are."
—Dan Millman, *Body, Mind Mastery*

Any dream or big goal begins with an honest look at your current life. It is important to gauge where you are right now. All of your experiences have brought you to this point. Each one has given you insight into your preferences, likes and dislikes, your strengths and weaknesses, your successes and failures. Each of these experiences provides valuable information about the skills you have. This also helps you decide what skills you will need to acquire and what additional changes you will have to make to accomplish your goal.

Borneo was my first international, high profile, adventure race (Eco-challenge, Borneo). I was fortunate to get on a sponsored team, as these races are pricey and hard to get into. The format was a ten day cut-off, which means that any team in danger of not completing the race within the ten day time period would be pulled from the course. The faster teams were expected to finish in seven or eight days. The race was non-stop around the clock. The disciplines were ocean paddling in native boats, running/trekking/jungle hiking, navigation, whitewater canoeing, caving, ascending/rappelling, ocean swimming, and mountain biking. With the hindsight of my adventure racing career, I can say with emphasis that this race was especially epic.

I think it is important to note that our team slept less than four hours at a shot for the nine days it took us to finish. This happened three or four times at best. We finished the morning of the ninth day in fifteenth place. Not bad for a rookie team. Eighty-five teams started this race, and around forty finished.

One vivid memory I have is of our first long jungle section. It was very humid and hot. I remember that I was constantly soaked with sweat. We had been racing about three days when we got to this section. There was no trail to speak of, only pink flagging through very dense jungle. We made our way from one bit of flagging to the next on steep, muddy, slick terrain using the branches to pull ourselves up the hills or slow ourselves down as we descended. Everything was thorny or prickly so my hands had gashes and cuts. We learned that due to the constant wetness nothing healed, so all wounds just got worse, and our skin was deteriorating (both feet and hands).

To add to the discomfort, whenever it started to rain the leeches would come to life jumping from branches or bushes onto us. I was horrified at first, then just plain angry at these repulsive little bloodsuckers. We had to be constantly removing them from our bodies. They even got into our shoes creating a mess with our feet. We were covered with mud, blood, and sweat by the time we reached our transition area, about two and a half days after entering this section of the race.

During this section we did try to sleep a bit both nights, since navigating the flagged route was almost impossible in the dark. However, the constant harassment from the leeches and the deafening sounds of the bugs, birds, and other wildlife, not to mention our bedding, which consisted of only a space blanket, made sleep elusive. When we did travel, we saw huge spiders, bird-sized bugs, monkeys, and baboons. These were constant reminders that we were not in North America.

I use this story as an example of an experience that prepared me for the rigors of Everest; it gave me a frame-work to refer to when I was pushed to what felt beyond my limits.

It is not always easy to look to the past when you are eager to get on with living your vision. However, a review of the past will help you steady your course, pace yourself, improve your skills, and give you a map to follow while summiting your dream mountain. It will also show the course corrections needed to change behaviors and patterns that are unproductive in achieving your goals. Remember, honesty about where you are starting, and where you have been, is essential.

When I was examining what it would take to get ready for the Mount Everest climb I had to be honest with myself about my fitness level, technical skills, and mental attitude. Because of my past experience in adventure racing I considered myself in excellent athletic condition. I had learned disciple. I had learned to keep a positive mental attitude and endure physical challenges.

The skills needed and acquired for the rigorous courses of adventure racing were a plus. However, when I began to look at what it would take to get myself in peak physical, mental, and emotional condition to confidently climb Mount Everest with its unpredictable weather, extreme temperatures, variable conditions, and dangerous terrain, I realized it was more than I had done to date.

In addition I would be outfitted with big boots, crampons, clumsy mitts, and an oxygen tank and mask while tackling many of these challenges. It felt overwhelming. I knew I had a great deal of work ahead of me to be prepared to complete the climb successfully.

One of the skills I needed to improve was my ability to clip and unclip from a fixed line, pass knots, and maneuver with accuracy and speed up and down the fixed line while my hands were encased in cumbersome, bulky climbing mitts. I knew that this would take a lot of practice.

My fitness level, which I thought was excellent, was not mountaineering-specific enough for me to climb Mount Everest. I had to evaluate my speed, strength, and endurance specifically for mountaineering as opposed to general overall fitness.

At first evaluation, I thought I was at least an "M" on a fitness scale from "A to Z." It wasn't long before I realized I was more like an "E." Becoming aware and being honest with myself made me even more determined to get the training I needed to move forward.

When I went to Alaska to climb Denali I had an eye-opening reality check. I was confident that this mountain would be no problem for me. The first five days went fairly easy. Then the reality of the expedition began to sink in. We were climbing with heavy loads and pulling sleds. The varying weather temperatures combined with the steep climbing experience on fixed line was a test of my strength, courage, and endurance.

After the fifth day, the climb continued to challenge me over and over again. I realized that what I had originally thought of as an "M" on the fitness scale of "A to Z" was, in truth, not exceeding a "D." At this moment I realized that I had less than a year to make major improvements in my fitness level. Being honest with myself was crucial and life saving.

Examining your current life and skill level will give you an idea, on a scale from "A to Z," of your current level—mentally, emotionally, and physically. As you begin to take steps toward your goal, you will need to continue to reevaluate where you are. Be bold enough to tell yourself the truth. In achieving goals there are no shortcuts. To succeed you will need your skill level at a "Z." For some, this will move along quickly, but for others it may take more time.

It is important to be very realistic with yourself about where you are in each of the areas that your goal requires a level of excellence, proficiency, and competence. If you are not sure, ask someone you trust to give you feedback. Before I left for Everest two of my coaches and mentors, who knew me from adventure racing, were willing to give me honest feedback on my skill level, fitness level, and mental fortitude. They both agreed, having seen me race, that I had what it takes, and they gave me ideas on ways to improve. I also knew intuitively where I was weak. It is often in the areas that we are most afraid of or avoid. Recognizing these areas is the first step in improving them.

When it comes to your goal, take all the steps you need to for success. Assess events from the past that will assist you in your goal. Be clear about your current place on the "A to Z" scale in every area of your plan. Begin the process of improving all the areas to become excellent, or at "Z," on the scale. These steps will insure your success.

Chapter Nine Exercises

Call to Action: Evaluating Where You Are

1. Make a list of your major accomplishments.

2. List the skills you have acquired that pertain to achieving your goals.

3. List the known skills you will need to develop to complete your goal.

Part III

Gearing Up

In the chapters of Part Three you will be challenged to look at your daily habits and to decide if you are willing to make needed shifts and changes in order to make room for new behaviors that support the success of your goal. Pace is another area that can greatly serve your progress. Go too slow, and you lose motivation and momentum; go too fast, and you can burn out. I like the affirmation "slow and steady," along with the insight that if speed is called for, I can shift into third gear and make it happen.

Gathering a support team that includes coaches or mentors is necessary. Look for those who have done what you want to do and who are willing to walk the miles with you. These teachers can be part of your over-all team. You may include a buddy that you are accountable to or a small group of trusted friends who believe in you and who will give you a boost when you're running out of steam.

Also, I can't stress enough how important some of the mental tools can be. It will be important for you to decide what works for you in this arena and make it a part of your daily or weekly action plan. Activities like visualizations, practice and focus, affirmations and quotes are powerful mental reinforces. Educating yourself is also valuable. Be an expert in your area of interest. This can be accomplished by reading books, listening to CDs, watching DVDs, and in some instances attending trainings, workshops, or seminars. As you have noted, I say over and over, take "one step at a time." All these things are steps moving you in a forward direction.

Finally, never underestimate the power of the looming storm, whatever this may mean for your personal goal. Perhaps you will get lucky and this event will never occur. I like to be prepared, and I encourage you to be prepared for the possibility. Remember, storms are designed to test your resolve and commitment to your vision. Fear is a factor to contend with when storms come. Keep it as far away as you can and be prepared for unknown obstacles.

10 | Prepare, Acclimate, and Pace

"We first make our habits and then our habits make us."
—John Dryden, *The Works of John Dryden*

Habits can help you succeed or contribute to your failure. Behaviors can focus your attention or scatter it. It is an important part of achieving any goal to have practices that fully support your efforts. Mediocrity and smallness will not fulfill a big goal. Commitment, consistency, and perseverance will.

Goals, large and small, will often require some change in current activities. For example, a new exercise program, a change in eating habits or sleeping routine, and beginning a meditation practice all require an examination of where you are now and where you want to be. Any lifestyle change will require small steps, small changes, and strategies to keep you on track and accountable.

When I look at what it will take to get ready for any physical goal, career goal, or a lifestyle change, I write down what I am currently doing, what I need to add to begin the process of getting closer to my destination, and what behaviors or habits I am currently engaged in that don't support my forward momentum. Once I get clear on my daily habits, I can implement small changes that support my progress. Writing down current patterns defines, with clarity, what I need to add or eliminate in order to create the change I desire.

When I was getting ready to launch my online maternity fitness clothing business I learned a great deal about focus and creating successful habits. Working at home afforded me tremendous flexibility, but it also required that I lose some habits that ate into the time I had available to work on my business. No longer could I spend as much time on personal matters, phone calls, emails, visits, etc. I realized how much of my day I had been devoting to these things, which is not bad; they just did not support my business.

What habits are you currently engaged in that distract you from your intention? You know what supports your new goal and what detracts from it. It is easy to make excuses for what you are doing and why you cannot make the change. It is crucial to reflect on this point. How strong is your commitment to modify your existing lifestyle?

An example of how people get sidelined from achieving their goals happened at a recent seminar I was facilitating. One participant said that she really wanted to start an exercise program but as the Vice President of a corporation she was struggling to find the time. My question to her was, "Do you have time to watch TV? Do you have to work ten to twelve hours a day or could you accomplish your work in eight to ten hours? What time do you get up in the morning? What can you cut out to make room for a fitness and health program?"

Triumph is not served by time wasters and bad habits. The tendency to normalize life in the humdrum of daily rituals will cause blinders, making it difficult to see how present habits eat away at the time and energy that could easily be applied to victory. The energy wasted could be used for learning new skills and implementing new programs to improve your chances of success.

Coffee is a habit of mine and affects the way I feel physically. I know that coffee consumption contributes to feeling edgy, crabby, and a little manic. It affects the way I perform. Other foods such as sugar and simple carbohydrates can be a quick-fix for your energy. However, in a short period of time they can leave you in a blood-sugar crash. This collapse can be self-defeating.

One of the habits I knew I needed to change in order to be at my peak performance to climb Mount Everest was in the area of diet. When I am physically pressed I tend to eat much less and forget to drink. This is a huge concern for anyone with goals that take a great deal of physical exertion. I had to create a new habit of eating and drinking whether or not I felt hunger or thirst. This took a fair amount of discipline.

Focus, perseverance, and discipline, specifically for climbing a big, hard mountain, involved a training routine. This was less of an issue for me since I had been training for one endurance sport or another for the past ten years. However, to get my physical endurance to a "Z," it took even more focus than ever before.

Changing habits and creating new behaviors is not easy. Changing all patterns at once is nearly impossible. It takes baby steps, one step at a time. Awareness of what you are or are not doing is the first step in changing bad habits and implementing new behaviors. It takes commitment to your goals. Success in one area will give you the experience of triumph and make the next lifestyle change easier. When I am wearing my hat as a fitness coach, I tell people that it takes about three months for a new behavior to become a habit. It is the same with setting a goal and taking all the steps necessary to accomplish it. It requires dedicated and ongoing persistence. Figure out what you're passionate enough about to create and stick to a plan. This is not something that will happen overnight. All I can say is breathe, and take the next step no matter how large or how small.

Another component of habits that create success is pace. We accomplish our big dreams and goals at very different paces. Writing a book is an example. A project like this might take one writer six months while it takes another writer three years. It is important to go at a pace that is neither too fast nor too slow for you.

Pace is the rate or speed you do something. Faster is not necessarily better. Taking it slow, one step at a time, in mountaineering, is the most prudent tempo to maintain unless an emergency occurs. If a crisis presents itself, swiftness may be needed in order to save lives. The perfect pace will take you to your destination.

Speed may be important in some big endeavors in order to accomplish success. There are many examples of this; in fact, for some people speed is a major part of accomplishing their big goal. In technical climbing or mountaineering, weather can force a speed that is beyond uncomfortable but that is necessary in order to stay safe or survive. Furthermore, some people are drawn to goals that require speed, like finishing a marathon in a certain time or making the cut-offs for a century bike ride. If you want to set a personal record as part of your goal then increasing speed would be included in your action plan.

I will never forget the humbling experience I had related to this idea of speed versus slow and steady. For the most part I had been one of the fastest trekkers in our group of twelve climbers. Some of us had moved at a breakneck pace during the acclimatizing trek to Base Camp on the south side, while others in the group had moved at a more moderate rate and a few people had trekked along rather slowly in my opinion. I was about to be in for a brutal surprise.

When we got to the north side in Tibet I was still in the mindset of moving as fast as possible to gain camps. Our first move was from Base Camp at 18,700 feet to Advanced Base Camp (ABC) at 21,000 feet. We all got up and left in the morning at about the same time. I and two others were soon leading the pack to the halfway point on this thirteen mile hike at around 20,000 feet. It was not long before I noticed that I was having a difficult time keeping the pace and my breathing was becoming more labored.

As I realized my dilemma, it became apparent that I was not going to be able to move at this speed for much longer. I was terrified that the group would notice my new acquired slowness and have less respect for me. In the end, camp came just in time, but the lesson had only begun.

The next day we all got on our way, and I was moving considerably slower than the day before. I was exhausted from my previous efforts to move faster than my body was comfortable moving, in fact I had put a lot of stress on myself physically by doing so. As I continued on to ABC things began to get really hard. I remember feeling like I had been hit by a Mack truck. My legs were moving at a snail's pace, I was gasping for air, and it was taking me forever to cover very little ground. Our expedition advisor noticed my struggle and stayed with me for the last 500 feet of climbing, encouraging me to keep going. When I arrived at ABC, I literally crawled to my tent and collapsed inside. I am sure the Sherpas in camp were less than impressed and concerned about this climber who they were going to be supporting on an attempt to summit Everest.

Going too fast, especially in the beginning phases of moving towards a goal, can lead to burnout. But if your pace is too slow, the possibility of losing motivation can occur and stop your progress. In sum, going either too fast or too slow can cause you to lose sight of your goal and invite failure.

My approach to most goals is slow and steady. I continue to take action daily. I do not stop. Keeping a constant pace I can maintain my energy and enthusiasm until the goal is achieved. I use the tool of pacing when guiding climbers to the top of mountains or trekking as well. The slow and steady approach has led to many successful climbs all the way to the top of mountains when all other conditions are in place. I recognize that it is important to be prepared to quicken the pace in climbing when weather threatens. Keeping a slow and steady tempo ensures a reserve of energy to sustain a faster speed when needed.

It is important to examine your goal realistically and to pick a pace that will sustain you. Stick with your plan. From time to time you may have to reevaluate your tempo. Are you staying consistent, or are you starting and stopping, losing momentum? Are you conserving your energy in the event you will need greater speed? Are you scattering your energy by going too slow? Do you need to pick up the pace or slow down? The consequences of being off pace can greatly impact the outcome you experience with your own goal. One of my most vivid memories related to pace occurred while guiding on Denali.

All was going as planned the first five days of a climbing expedition I was assisting on Denali. We were gaining an elevation of 1,000 to 2,000 feet per day which is a perfect pace. We arrived at Base Camp, which is at 14,000 feet, as a storm was hitting. For two days the winter storm dumped several inches of snow. The third day the weather cleared. We waited for another twenty-four hours for the snow to settle and for the avalanche hazard to reduce before resuming our schedule of moving up the mountain. On the fourth day we began the slog up the headwall carrying a heavy load of supplies for high camp. As we were plodding along we heard a huge crash overhead. I saw a wall of snow headed in our direction. "Run!!!!" the lead guide Scott Woolums shouted.

Our group of four, roped together and carrying heavy packs, raced sideways as fast as we could through eight inches of freshly fallen snow. The avalanche stopped just short of us; however, we were hit with the blow down or wall of loose, powdery snow. This was an emergency situation where great speed was needed and there was no time to waste. While this example is dramatic it does put value on the requirement for urgency.

Pace is a tool with a wide spectrum of applications. At different junctures in your journey you will need to reevaluate your pace. Staying present to the demands of circumstances along the way will assist you in correcting the speed at which you are moving. Be prepared for the obvious and for events that are not apparent at the moment. Stay flexible, consistent, on course, and prepared. Keep in mind speed is not always what is needed. Sometimes patience takes its place, and, as we know, patience is not always swift.

As you fine tune your plan be sure to clearly evaluate any habits you can add or eliminate. Be prepared to continually assess your pace and adjust it as needed.

Chapter Ten Exercises

Call to Action: Habits for Success

1. Write a list of your current habits and note how much time you engage in each of them. (For example, watching television two hours in the evening, drinking five cups of coffee per day, exercising one time per week, etc.)

2. Which of these habits support your goals and which ones don't?

3. What new habits are you willing to put into practice today that will support your objective?

4. Evaluate your goal. What pace will serve you in the beginning stages as you begin to take action?

5. Take time to envision your goal all the way to completion. Are there times that you are aware of right now that you will need to pick up the pace or slow down?

6. What is your strategy for handling emergencies or urgent situations along the way when speed is needed? Does your pace support you in conserving enough energy for unforeseen obstacles?

11 | Support Team

"Luck is a matter of preparation meeting opportunity."
—Oprah Winfrey, *Oprah Magazine*

Arming yourself with as many tools and strategies as possible is a necessary step for achieving your goals. There is no reason to "reinvent the wheel." There is so much to gain from others' experiences, especially those who have achieved what you want to attain. That is why having a coach or mentor is important.

When I was still in my decision process around whether or not to climb Everest one of the first things I did was contact three people that had climbed the North Route; they knew me and had a pretty good idea of my skill level. All were people I greatly respected. I will never forget how shocked and grateful I was when my now close friend Ellen Miller called me from Katmandu after receiving an email from me asking her what she thought about my idea to climb. She had just finished a trek in the area. She could have just shot me back a quick email but true to who she is she felt a huge need to check my level of commitment, challenge my beliefs surrounding the difficulty, and offer support only if I was truly committed on all levels. This included my ability to turn around if circumstances, conditions, or the mountain warranted it. She was to become one of my most powerful supports on this journey, and is a true friend to this day.

My personal formula for success begins with creating my team. It could be a combination of coaches, mentors, or friends. It is important to be discriminating in your choice. Negative opinions of others can stop a goal in its tracks. Choose people who have successfully accomplished what you seek to achieve and who believe in your success. I cannot stress this enough. These choices will help you fill your pack with the essentials.

When I was making my plan to climb Mount Everest my coaches and mentors were key to my success and safety. Initially I went to three individuals looking for some guidance and support. As I had been discouraged from even trying to climb based on a few opinions I had already received, I was learning to be careful of who I now chose to share this dream with. There were those who believed I had no business attempting the climb. They felt I did not have the skills, physical endurance, or experience necessary for a safe and successful trip. These opinions did not sway me from my vision, and these were not the people I chose to be on my team. As a matter of fact, it made me more determined to do what I needed to do in order to climb that mountain.

I recognized right up front that if I was going to achieve my goal I needed to be very discriminating with whom I shared my action plan. I got in the habit of sharing with people that I could count on for direction and advice and who were fully supportive of my ambition. I chose positive thinkers who were in no way threatened by the big picture.

An important guideline that I used in creating this team was that the people I chose needed to be experts in the area I was about to immerse myself in. My approach was to email them with a request for a telephone follow-up. I asked them if they would be open to providing a realistic picture of what I could expect on the climb and to explore their opinions of my abilities in relation to this endeavor. This is a step that I find necessary for success. Find yourself at least one person that can encourage you and help you honestly evaluate where you are and what your next steps need to be. If at all possible, make sure they have done what you want to do.

The three coaches and mentors I talked with gave me valuable insight into designing the rest of my plan. They gave me a good picture of what to expect physically, what challenges to prepare for, and what to expect mentally. They also explained logistic considerations, including how to involve family members, friends, the local fund-raising and support team, and so much more.

I began to surround myself with a group of people from the local community and beyond who believed in me and my aspiration. They became a very small circle of support that made my success possible during those many moments when the whole idea seemed impossible or improbable. I will never forget a pivotal point in my climb when this circle of support helped me jump off the cliff, so to speak.

It was May 20. There had already been nine fatalities during the climbing season. Most of the recent deaths had occurred on the North Col Route. Our team was getting ready to attempt the summit. The weather was looking ominous. In climbing terms, to move forward at this point was called "going up stairs" or moving into the death zone. I was on the fence about whether or not to proceed. I was scared, mentally worn down, and physically tired from the ascent. Waiting for the weather window was uncomfortable. The truth is, I just wanted to get the climb over with and go home. I had had just about enough.

Knowing I had a dynamite support team back home was invaluable. I emailed a couple of people from my community team, expressing all the doubts, fears, and concerns related to moving up the mountain. The responses I received ranged from "You can do it!" and "Give it a try," to "You can turn around if things look bad!" I desperately needed to hear these words of encouragement and to know that there were people out there who really believed in me and trusted my judgment.

These people encouraged me to move past my fear and go for the accomplishment of my dream. I have one short email that demonstrates this point. On May 27 I responded to my friend and constant support, Lauren Miller, with this message "Lauren, It was quite a journey and I am finally down to ABC which is considered a safe zone. I felt all the support the five days I was in the danger zone, so to speak, and just kept taking one step at a time as long as it felt right. I love you all and will be home soon. Love Laurie."

I cannot stress enough that we don't accomplish big goals on our own. It is always a group effort. Gather your team. It could be one coach or mentor. It could be a supportive friend or family member. It could a combination of these people, and if at possible have someone on board who has done what you want to do. Doing this will forever change the way you view accomplishing the big challenges in your life.

Chapter Eleven Exercises

Call to Action: Coaches and Mentors

1. Who currently supports you most in your success? Who is unsupportive of you?

2. Begin to formulate your positive support team. Who will you invite to be a part of your group?

3. Who do you currently know that has done what you want to accomplish? If you do not know anyone who has done what you are setting out to achieve, who do you know that knows someone? Get the telephone number and/or email address of the person/s and contact them. Begin asking questions pertinent to your endeavor.

12 | What to Pack

"This thing that you want, see it, feel it, and believe in it. Make your mental blueprint and begin to build."
—Robert Collier, www.braineyquote.com

Visualizations are done with a positive attitude. You use them to focus on getting through the hard parts of the journey to reach your desired outcomes. Visualization will strengthen your confidence to overcome what lies ahead. It can be like gold and create an energy that moves you past obstacles with a greater ease and comfort.

I use visualizations on a regular basis when getting ready for big events and competitions. When I was mountain-bike racing, I would go off on my bike for a slow warm-up prior to the race. I would listen to motivational music and imagine myself maneuvering the race course with ease. I would picture myself effortlessly managing the challenging parts of the course, especially the climbs, completing the mental picture with a victorious crossing of the finish line, feeling excellent about my performance. If I was on an unfamiliar race course and unsure of what obstacles I would be experience along the way, I would envision myself on a generic course and always end the visualization with a successful conclusion and feeling of triumph. I encourage you to use this tool to support your forward momentum.

One of my most powerful experiences using a visualization process was the birth of my daughter Avriel. Prior to her delivery I went to childbirth classes that guided her father and me through the process of breathing, focusing, and pain management (if there is such a thing during labor, especially if you choose to go drug free). I spent months before her arrival visualizing and preparing for her birth. I can say that in my labor experience the real thing was much more encompassing than my visualizations leading up to the event. However, I believe this exercise helped me get through some of my fear related to the pain I experienced during labor. You will need to come up with your own picture of success. What do you want to see, feel, and experience as you journey towards your goals?

What things do you see yourself needing to overcome? I believe in any big vision there will always be aspects that are scary and need to be worked with. Maybe some of your plan requires you to explore new, unknown territory.

Prior to climbing Mount Everest, I committed to the habit of visualizing my success. I did this in relation to managing the expedition route physically, mentally, and emotionally. I had to rely on pictures, old video clips, and book descriptions of the route, especially the Second Step which is one of the most dangerous sections of the climb. I would do this practice at least twice a week while sitting quietly in a meditative state. Each time I visualized myself successfully making it all the way to the summit and back safely.

I also began to practice calming myself down from a place of panic. It was easy for me to imagine what could go wrong along the way. I had heard of many challenges that were ahead. I needed to be mentally prepared. This habit of feeling myself in a state of panic and then calming myself down became invaluable during my climbing experiences both ascending and descending the mountain. I have used this same technique to get myself prepared to speak or present. I visualize myself delivering a wonderful presentation with lots of clapping as opposed to focusing on all the things that could go wrong.

Beginning this practice may feel a bit awkward. I recommend finding yourself a quiet place where you can sit comfortably for at least five minutes two or three times a week. I sometimes light a candle to change the energy around me. I spend a minute or so just getting calm and relaxed with smooth even breaths. Once I am in this state of mind I think about what it is I want to accomplish or create. The more detail you can bring to this practice the better. The longer you can hold the visualization the better.

Don't worry if you are able to do this for only a few minutes. Over time many people develop the skill to hold their visualizations for five minutes or longer. The practice of visualization is a success tool. Place yourself in a winner's position. See the vision all the way to a successful climax and beyond.

Another tool that I have found helpful is one-pointed focus, or to be exact, developing the discipline of focus. This became a living, breathing mantra throughout all of my training. It was a discipline that took me to the finish line in adventure racing and all the way to the summit and back. Without the discipline of focusing my energy, my success would have been limited. What you need to consider is the universal law, "What we dwell upon grows." What are you thinking about, putting time and energy into, spending time on? If it is not your goal, then you may want to reevaluate the goal you have chosen or refocus your intention.

When I first began my training and research for the Everest climb I was put in touch with a Sherpa named Hooman Aprin. He supported a group of western climbers including the third United States woman to summit in 2001. His mantra to me was, "Be calm, focused, and relentless on the climb." His story is as follows. He said he was part of the team of Sherpas fixing the lines for all the climbers on the south route that season.

This team goes up the mountain every year in the worst weather conditions to fix the lines before the summit bids can move forward. The Sherpas also face great danger. They have to belay one another and travel without fixed lines for the duration of the climb to the summit. Hooman told me that his one concern is always to make sure everything was done flawlessly. This was his strategy that was designed to maintain safety for the climbers coming up the mountain as well as for his own team members. Focusing on safety allowed him to think of only the next step in front of him, the next piece of protection that needed to be placed, or the Sherpa in front of or behind him who might need support. Hooman said that he was not even aware that he was approaching the summit until he was almost there. With winds blowing forty to fifty miles per hour and temps at minus fifty, this is truly a story of relentless focus.

The dictionary definition for discipline means "to train or develop by instruction and exercise." Focus takes training and practice. I am often asked, "How do you develop the discipline of focus?"

As a fitness coach I use a formula with clients that begins with a series of questions to clarify their goals. I have them rate their commitment level on a scale of one to ten, ten being fully committed. Their commitment must be high in order to succeed. Then I ask them the following questions: Why do you want to make this life-style change? What do you enjoy doing in relationship to fitness (this could be dancing, rollerblading, walking, etc.)? What big goal could you work towards accomplishing within six months? What is a smaller goal that you feel you could accomplish in three months that would move you closer to your ultimate goal? Are you willing to be accountable to me at least once a week?

Once we have gone through this process of identification and clarification, I work to design a program that the client is ultimately responsible for. A willingness to be responsible for your plan is the first step in discipline and it is prerequisite to learning the skill of focus. Then it becomes a process of creating accountability, developing a plan that the client is committed to, and finally developing a back-up plan should adversity show up.

Once the primary plan and a back-up plan are in place, it becomes easier to flow through your day with calm discipline and focus. When your world falls apart, the discipline and focus will keep you on track to create the lifestyle change that leads to achieving the goal you desire.

Chapter Twelve Exercises

Call to Action: Visualization and Focus

1. Research your goal. Begin to find out as much as you can about the direction you are taking. Write a description of your course.

2. Think about your goal. Begin the mind journey of visualization. Explore every nuance of your goal and direct the expedition in your mind as the perfect scenario with a victorious conclusion.

3. As you become clearer, your visualizations will become clearer. The clearer you become, the easier it will be to visualize yourself summiting your dream mountain and returning home safely. Practice honing your visualization to reach your goal.

4. What is your commitment level to your goal on a scale of 1 to 10?

5. Why do you want to achieve this goal?

6. What discipline do you need to develop in order to focus and stay on track?

7. Who are you willing to be accountable to?

13 | Habits for Success

"Tell me and I'll forget. Show me and I may remember. Involve me, and I'll understand."
—Native American Saying

I highly recommend educational tools to anyone wanting to accomplish any goal, large or small. Education, knowledge, and wisdom are essential for preparing, training, and completing any endeavor. Become an expert in the area that you want to excel in. Books, CDs and DVDs pertaining to your mission are fabulous; however, do not overlook inspirational and motivational materials as part of what is in your pack. Attending conferences, workshops, or events that are specific to what you want to learn more about is also important. Coming into contact with the experts in your area of focus is powerful! To make it to the zenith you will need the whole package—education, knowledge, wisdom, motivation, and inspiration.

When I began my business, Life Journeys, and started exploring how to present the art of goal setting to people, I spent hours reading books written by respected business people in the field, everyone from Dale Carnegie to Suze Orman. I also made it a practice to listen to CDs while I was doing housework or driving. I chose material that was interesting and helped me decide how I wanted to reach people and help them access their passions, gifts, and dreams. Reading and listening to CDs made a huge difference in my knowledge base. This alone helped me sift through lots of ideas, experiences, and advice and in order to pull together the pieces that made the most sense to me. You will need to do some research to figure out which tools best serve you and you will need to decide what you are willing to commit to in your quest to realize your vision.

With the Everest goal I read every book I could get my hands on about climbing this mountain. Most of the books were non-fiction, but even fiction books on the subject had many elements of truth in them. I also watched videos and DVDs that showed people climbing the North Col Route, which was the route I would be climbing. Witnessing what people had to endure no matter what route they were climbing on Everest was very helpful for my mental preparation. Anything you can do to become more focused and knowledgeable about your goal will move you one step closer to actualizing it. Knowledge is power.

There are two other tools that I use to motivate and inspire me: affirmations and quotes. Both of these are very personal and have the most power when you choose those that speak directly to you. Affirmations are best stated in the present tense. They should not include words like: should, don't, can't, and have to. Always keep your affirmations positive. Be direct in your affirmations. Claim that which you are affirming right here, right now. Statements like "I am" and "I have" are very effective. In cases where you are preparing for something that has a deadline, you can make an affirmation like, "I will be ready by such and such a date."

Affirmations I used daily in preparing for my climb were:

- "I am ready for Everest by May of 2006 and if the stars align I will go for the top."

- "I am prepared for this journey. I will listen to the mountain's warnings at all times. Get in, get up, and get out!"

Two quotes that inspired me for my journey were from a friend, Doug Carter:

- "There are no short cuts," and

- "All I ever have to do is take the very next step."

Another quote that I apply to all areas of my life is: "One step at a time." This is an additional tool that I use while moving towards my goal.

I have also found that music can be a huge motivator. I lean towards music that has meaningful or inspiring lyrics. One of my favorite picks is a CD of chanting from Nepal.

In the climbing world we use the term "acclimate," which means to give your body a chance to get used to the elevation. In a perfect ascent there would be a gain of a thousand feet of elevation per day. Small steps equal big gains over a period of time; therefore, "one step at a time" gets you to the goal. As you move for-

ward on your path, keep all your tools handy and remember to draw on whatever tool or strategy you need
as you need it.

An experience I had during my adventure racing career demonstrates this one step at a time attitude; it
also shows the importance of using additional tools.
The eco challenge in New Zealand was my third long
format adventure race, which means that the race was
expected to last for at least six days for the fast teams
with a cut-off of ten days for all teams. Again, our team
finished in the top twenty racing against the best teams
in the world. This race taught me the importance of
urgency and perseverance in several situations. About
half-way through the race, we had a 125 mile mountain-bike section, which we were told we could ride for
the most part (later I wondered by who?).

We started off on fairly friendly terrain, decent
weather, no mishaps. About thirty to forty miles in, our
team noticed two things, a brewing storm and a huge
climb. By now we had been riding most of the day,
and it was approaching late afternoon. We started up
the steep terrain only to find ourselves barely able to
push our bikes at times, it was that steep. I think the
climb was twenty-five to thirty miles. Needless to say,
we were pushing or riding super slow due to the gradi-
ent of the climb. On top of that the storm was building. We had been warned about the electrical storms
in New Zealand, specifically the danger it presented on
the ridge, which we would gain at the end of the climb.
Rumor had it that teams that did not make the ridge
before the storm hit would be stopped and held until
the storm had passed.

We were on a mission to avoid any delays. After hours of pushing and riding as fast as we could, we reached the top of the climb before the storm hit. By now it was night, dark, and I was exhausted. As we started down the other side of the climb I noticed, as did my teammates, that I was having a hard time negotiating the road. I kept steering off, falling asleep, and could not focus. My depth perception was shot. This was scary as I could have ridden off the road and had a serious injury. We did make it to the bottom of the descent and opted for a few hours rest until daylight. I do remember that it was so cold it was hard to sleep for long. Space blankets are not exactly luxury, and they were the only warm item we carried on this leg of the race. My experience taught me the role that urgency can play in accomplishing a goal, and it showed me how perseverance is key to long term success. The gift is to know when to do what, and to keep taking the right steps.

As you acclimate to your new plan, tools, and strategies it is important to apply the "one day at a time" or "one step at a time" philosophy. Going too fast can cause burn-out; going too slow you may lose the ability to stay focused. Acclimate a day at a time, always taking at least one action per day. Day after day those baby steps turn into quantum leaps. "An overnight success takes about ten years" or so the saying goes. So, pace yourself.

It has become part of my morning routine to review my goals and plans for the day. I always double check that I am taking at least one step that day that will support two to four of my goals. This keeps me focused and gives me a sense of accomplishment even if my actions are small. I also make sure that I am reading or listening to something that enhances my knowledge base. In addition, I plan a time each morning to review and repeat my affirmations and quotes. Figure out what works best for you. We are all different, but I encourage you to create a lifestyle change that leaves the space for these supportive activities and strategies.

Chapter Thirteen Exercises

Call to Action: Tools and Strategies for Success

1. Begin to accumulate educational materials on your topic; borrow from friends, visit the library, research books, tapes, CDs, and DVDs online. Begin to amass knowledge and wisdom on achieving expertise in your goal.

2. Who inspires and motivates you? What music moves you and helps you stay calm and centered? Begin to listen to lectures or inspiring music and read more of the material that supports your growth.

3. Begin to create positive affirmations that keep you focused on success. Collect quotes that speak to you. Post the affirmations and quotes where you can see them frequently. Read them and say them out loud to yourself daily.

14 | When the Storm Hits

"Obstacles don't have to stop you. If you run into a wall don't turn around and give up. Figure out how to climb it, go through it or work around it."
—Michael Jordan

Storms are a given. They are the obstacles that threaten to halt your progress. In order to achieve your goals you will need tools to overcome blocks and hardships. Building your abilities to manage smaller adversities will give you the confidence and practice that will strengthen your ability to go beyond larger barriers.

A few months ago a very good friend and support person reminded me that adversity is designed to test your resolve. She had sent me some old emails from our correspondence right before our summit attempt. It reminded me of what I was experiencing at that moment and how her help had moved me through the brick wall that seemed to be in the way. I felt that the correspondence was very appropriate for this chapter.

I emailed her, "Hi Lauren, we are getting our group ready for the summit push and I am feeling pretty scared right now. I am just ready to get this thing over with and come home. Sadly the weather does not look good for awhile or rather the winds are just too high. Some groups have gone anyway and there have been tons of cases of frostbite and four deaths in the past three days. We had four members of our team try and all four turned back due to the high winds. I am just glad they are safe. Mother Nature will decide what is next and in the meantime we are all ready to go. With much Love Laurie."

Lauren wrote back, "We are all holding you here in our thoughts and prayers. Remember how hard you have worked. If it makes any difference I say go for it!!"

To which I responded, "So good to hear all this. What did not come through on the project Himalaya video clip was that two of their members almost died. One was almost left for dead just below the summit because he could not walk. Only drugs, Sherpa support and lot of oxygen saved him. Our group was involved in the rescue. They used all our Sherpas and some of our O2. The rescue did not end until late last night (around 12 A.M.). I was down in Project Himalayas camp today assisting the guy that almost died. He was so exhausted he could not walk or eat, plus he had bad frostbite on his hands and feet. I am just so glad all the members are back safe. We have a summit window now and will be leaving for the top either the 22nd or the 23rd. I will keep you all posted. I am so grateful for all the support and prayers. I have not decided if I will go above Camp Three. I am taking one thing at a time. I need to come home to all who love me. Love Laurie."

I have found that the bigger your goal is the more adversity you are likely to experience. It may show up in the form of negativity or lack of support from family members or other people in your life. Adversity can also come in the form of politics and red tape. Education or lack thereof may also be a factor. A number of things can become an obstruction to your goal. There are unknown obstacles that will present themselves along the journey. It is important to consider the known difficulties that you will face and prepare for the unidentified problems. Set tools in place to deal with them as they come up. Be prepared so that when adversity hits you are ready for it.

Fear is a road block that must be recognized and dealt with. Personal fear can stop you from accomplishing your objective. It can take many forms, such as fear of success, fear of failure, fear of rejection, fear of change, just to name a few.

You will recognize personal fear by its power to derail you and/or stop you in your tracks. You will begin to avoid or resist doing what is needed to move you closer to your aspiration. The word fear means to pass through. Have a plan to deal with personal fear immediately. Find the tools that work for you to push you past it, find a way around it or through it. Each time you succeed in overcoming your personal fear you will increase your confidence and determination to complete your goal. In my experience fear accompanies big visions. The key is to be prepared for it, address it, and to continue forward in spite of it.

When I decided to climb the North Col Route of Mount

Everest, I knew I would have to negotiate a fair amount of exposure and technical climbing. I felt fear and panic around both. To navigate my trepidation, I made a commitment to myself to do the thing that I dreaded and feared the most. I made a plan and stuck to it. Once a week I drove a total of three hours to a climbing gym to improve my technical climbing skills and to work on overcoming my fear of exposure. This strategy paid off. As I did the things that terrified me the most I became more comfortable in my abilities and learned how to control my panic. It was essential for my security and success to push through my fears and just do it. The end result took me to the summit and brought me home safely.

Storms are a part of life. Accepting them and preparing for them with tools of empowerment will encourage you to continue your journey and to succeed. One thing I teach people is to expect the storms and obstacles. If possible, anticipate them so that when they arrive you are stronger and more prepared to go the distance. If there is one thing you can count on it is that obstacles will show up at some point on your journey.

Chapter Fourteen Exercises

Call to Action: What to Do When the Storm Hits

1. What are the obvious obstacles to your goal?

2. What personal fears lurk around your goal?

3. What tools will you need to move beyond these challenges? Begin to put these strategies into practice today.

Part IV

Success One Step at a Time

In this last part you will have a chance to examine your current beliefs around topics relevant to your vision. This is the time to decide if they are serving you or if you are ready to do something different. Red flags happen on anyone's climb. They are a warning that you need to make a decision. What is your current strategy when this happens? Do you give yourself some time to consider your options, or do you jump in and make a decision right away.

A related issue is the fact that you will also encounter daily adversity. By creating a Plan A and a Plan B you set yourself up to shift gears when something unexpected shows up, despite your careful planning.

Another consideration on your journey to the top is noticing the changing views as you progress ever closer to your goal. Most of what you will learn is not on the summit but in all that happens on your way there. As you complete your journey and accomplish what you have worked so hard for, you may find yourself wondering what is next.

Not to worry, the accomplishment of something big

is bound to change you in ways you cannot imagine. There will be new ways that you to look at what you now consider to be motivating and inspiring. These new ways may very well be 180 degrees from where you have just been.

Finally, there are new realms that open up. How do you adventure into the unknown? Venturing into the uncharted, like jumping off the cliff, is best done when you feel held and supported. Adventuring into new realms will now be much easier. You know how to put things into play that support your new path.

15 | Recognizing Red Flags

"The term red flag is used to describe something that is going wrong fast."
—Laurie Bagley

A red flag, in climbing terms, refers to something that is not going well. It could be weather, a problem with gear, the terrain, or a physical issue, such as injury or illness. Most climbers consider three red flags as an indication to abort a summit attempt. There are many famous stories of people that did not follow this formula with disastrous results, often ending in physical death. The most written about example was the 1996 climbing season. This is often referred to as the "Into Thin Air" season. It received this name from the famous book that told the story of eight climbers who died in a two day period because they did not heed the weather warnings, turn around in time, or pay attention to the signs of serious fatigue and illness. Any one of these would be considered a red flag.

As you navigate your path, red flags will reflect your challenges. Don't underestimate their power. Be looking for signs that a problem is developing. If your awareness is focused on your efforts, you may be able to head off a potentially serious situation before it affects your desired outcome.

On my Mount Everest journey, I had decided that if there was just one red flag, I would consider terminating my summit attempt and return to Advanced Base Camp. What could have been considered a red flag was an experience I had on the day we were going to attempt to summit. We were at Camp Two, which is at 25,500 feet. This was my first experience using oxygen. I had no prior practice of using an oxygen mask, which at first felt suffocating and restricting. Furthermore, it made me feel like I was wearing blinders and sorely limited my visual field. Then I discovered that this life-saving mask caused my goggles to fog up, restricting my vision even more. This was enough to cause me to panic and breathe heavily, which uses oxygen at a much greater rate. I did not realize how cumbersome and disorienting it would be to climb without the ability to see my feet. My capacity to clip and unclip from the fixed line was reduced and visibility became very difficult. I felt clumsy, awkward, and slow. This was a bad combination.

Everything I did in the first thirty minutes was painfully difficult. I felt like I was moving in slow motion. During this time I was sure I would need to turn back. If I was to proceed, I knew I would have to learn a new way of navigating every step and every action. At this snail's pace, which was dangerous, I knew I did not stand a chance of summiting. The question in my mind was, "Is this a red flag, one that would warrant my turning around?"

I decided to continue. I gave myself thirty more minutes to become more proficient and automatic. Within fifteen minutes things began to shift. The walking got easier and my pace quickened. I became faster at clipping and unclipping from the fixed line. I became accustomed to having my face covered by the oxygen mask. I learned how to manage the problem of my goggles fogging up. My breathing slowed down which created a feeling of calmness that allowed me to keep going.

I believe that whenever it is possible, it is important to give yourself a little time to decide how to respond rather than to react immediately to a red flag. Giving yourself time, another fifteen minutes or even twenty-four hours, can dramatically alter the outcome of any situation that presents itself.

To navigate and have successful outcomes in red flag situations, I have found having a Plan B to be helpful. I think through possible adversities and make a plan of response. I also visualize positive outcomes. This enables me to feel prepared rather than overwhelmed and panicked in adverse circumstances.

While preparing for the Mount Everest climb, I visualized positive outcomes and route negotiation. I knew that certain sections of the route would be difficult for me. I also knew that weather on the mountain could be problematic. Equipment challenges and equipment failures needed to be considered. I spent some time thinking about how I would handle each of the possible difficulties and my responses to adversity. This gave me a sense of preparedness. As you move forward on your path, keep a plan for red flags close at hand.

Keep in mind some red flags are just warnings meant to sharpen your awareness. Others may give you information that requires a new or revised plan.

It was the day of our summit success. Nema and I were the first of our party to reach the top of the mountain. The other members of our group were only minutes behind us. After we had been on top of the world for a brief twenty minutes our expedition advisor, Scott Woolums, looked at my oxygen gauge and noticed that I had two bars left, which meant that I only had twenty to twenty-five minutes of oxygen in my tank. My spare bottle of oxygen was at the top of the Second Step which was a frightening forty to forty-five minutes away. At this altitude, the one thing you don't want to do is run out of oxygen. Upon hearing the news, I knew the possibility loomed. I was terrified of the prospect of being out of oxygen for at least twenty minutes before I reached the top of the Second Step where my spare was waiting.

Nema and I wasted no time getting our descent underway. At first I remember feeling nothing but sheer panic. My breathing increased which meant I was using more oxygen and that limited my supply further. I had thought through this situation prior to the climb and had made a Plan B. Being prepared for such an obstacle helped me implement this plan. I knew I had twenty to twenty-five minutes to descend as fast and as far as I could. If the oxygen ran out, and if the terrain would allow, my plan was that Nema and I could share his oxygen mask. If the worst case scenario happened, I would sit down, which requires less oxygen, and wait for Nema to bring me the spare bottle. Because I was prepared, I was able to calm myself and slow my breathing. Staying calm, I navigated the tricky and treacherous summit pinnacle, summit traverse, and Third Step before my oxygen ran out. This was a red flag that turned out not to be a show-stopper this time.

Red flags are going to happen. How will you respond? Will you react in fear, or will you respond with awareness and preparedness? Think through, from beginning to end, the possible challenges you may encounter along the way. If a red flag shows up, visualize the positive outcome you desire.

It is true that some situations cannot be anticipated and come as a total surprise. In times like these, reacting may be the only thing you can do. If at all possible, give yourself a little more time to think through the circumstance so that you can respond in a manner that supports your success.

Chapter Fifteen Exercises

Call to Action: Recognizing Red Flags

1. What are the possible red flags you might encounter during your climb to success? Make a list.

2. Think through these possible adverse situations. What can you do to support yourself while deciding on a plan of action?

3. Visualize total success, best case scenario, in the accomplishment of your goal. Continue to practice this visualization throughout your journey.

16 | Daily Adversity

"Nothing great was ever done without much enduring."
—Catherine of Siena, *Her Mysticism—Drawn by Love*

When I was preparing for my expedition to Mount Everest, one of the most challenging obstacles for me came in the form of criticism from people I knew and sometimes from people I didn't know. People are often eager to share their doubts, fears, and skepticism with those willing to take risks to accomplish big goals. Those judgments can stop you in your tracks if you do not have a plan to deal with them. I have found that adopting the attitude that their opinions were just that —simply opinions—was a step in the right direction. I knew what I wanted and others' thoughts and beliefs would not get in my way of success.

On the actual climb, I physically faced daily adversity in many forms. High altitudes mixed with subzero temperatures and wind, of any velocity, can cause extreme cold. When the sky clears and the sun comes out it becomes exceptionally hot. These extreme temperature variations are difficult adjustments for the body to make—freezing one moment and sweating the next.

On another note, with all the protective clothing I needed to wear the inconvenience of having to use a relatively small pee bottle to urinate in was clumsy, to say the least. The bottle had to be taken outside and dumped immediately to prevent the urine from freezing in it, which at below zero temperatures could happen quickly. If you made the mistake of forgetting to empty your bottle you would have the misfortune of having to carry it to the next camp (extra weight) and hope that it would melt along the way.

A challenge I also faced was the inability to breathe with ease above 20,000 feet. It is hard to imagine, but especially at night I felt like I was constantly suffocating. Also, at this elevation the body no longer has enough oxygen to heal itself. To protect the cuts I had acquired on my fingers due to the cold (extremely cold weather causes skin to split and crack) my hands had to be duct taped. These examples merely scratch the surface. Physically, every day there were always more challenges to overcome on the mountain.

The daily emotional and mental tests were also present. I am a person of action. I was born to move my body. My mind is quick and structured and always ready for the next step. Inactivity tends to test my patience. I faced boredom on the mountain when we were forced to wait on weather windows. I was missing my daughter and in idleness found myself worrying about how she was doing. She knew there was a chance that I might not return. I knew that there was a chance that I wouldn't return, yet we both were hoping for the best possible outcome. And, as often is the case with groups, there were negative group dynamics to contend with. Mentally and emotionally I worked hard to keep myself in check. To do otherwise could cause bigger issues to arise.

Learning to overcome daily adversity is a part of everyday life. Becoming skillful in your ability to manage smaller hardships will give you the confidence and practice that will strengthen your ability to face and conquer the larger obstacles. Daily adversity can be anything from running out of gas or being late for a meeting to getting a call from your child's principal. It can be as simple as getting a run in your stockings just before a big presentation or having your children make a mess in the house just before company arrives. Another form   daily adversity takes is other people's unrealistic expectations, criticisms, or negative emotions. How do you handle the little challenges that present themselves on a daily basis?

Becoming aware of how you handle daily adversity now will give you an overall picture of how you will handle big obstacles. Your behavior around the little things is a magnifying glass for the larger challenges. Do you use coping mechanisms such as avoidance, excuses, or procrastination? Do you medicate with food or alcohol? Do you flip on the television set or computer and numb out? Do you blow up in anger and frustration, yelling and screaming uncontrollably? Do you go into denial and shut down? Do you deal with each life experience in the moment in a take-charge or controlling way? Knowing your current style will help you decide if you need to make changes. Taking action to reevaluate how you deal with the little things will encourage successful maneuvering with the larger upsets in life.

There are many different ways to be proactive when it comes to preparing for daily adversity. The system I utilize in my life involves writing out my daily plan the night before. I use three categories to organize my upcoming day: urgent and important, important, and urgent but not important. With my plan firmly in mind I am prepared for anything that comes up that will require a change in my schedule. This does not mean my day proceeds like clockwork. If I am only able to accomplish the urgent and important items on my list I reprioritize for the next day. Again, I think a key component to any system you use is planning ahead, staying flexible, and having a Plan B if your Plan A falls apart.

It is often challenging to distinguish between those things that are urgent and important and urgent but not important. Through practice this distinction will become easier. A question that will help you clarify the difference is: Who is this urgent for? Be clear and honest with yourself. It is not necessary to drop everything and take on the emergencies that belong to others. If it is not urgent for you, then decide when you want to deal with the matter.

Daily adversity will often test your commitment to your goals. Your willingness to stay on course when events threaten to get in the way will instill confidence and add to your momentum. Do these daily tests throw you off course or do you have the dedication that it takes to persevere and move forward?

It has been my experience that very few days go exactly as I had planned. Over time I have become comfortable with the strategies mentioned above which help me stay in balance and calm in the face of change. I think one of my biggest teachers in this regard was the birth of my daughter. In the beginning, I would become frustrated and angry when things did not even come close to following my plan. Her nursing schedule, sleep patterns, medical challenges, and my newness to mothering made life seem very off balance and chaotic. The first year of her life taught me the power and necessity of having a plan to deal with daily adversity. It also helped me learn to be willing to change my plan to incorporate what she needed. Over time, since I had a Plan B, I became less angry or frustrated when my day changed to accommodate what I could not have predicted.

In addition to dealing with identified obstacles and possible adversities there are also the giant curve balls of life that come out of nowhere. For example, when my daughter Avriel was three weeks old, she was diagnosed with a syndrome that required open heart surgery. Without the surgery her life expectancy was less then six months. As a new mother, I was beyond distraught. I developed strategies to stay strong and focused through my daughter's diagnosis, surgery, and ultimate recovery, and I have continued to rely on these strategies until today.

First, I created a small, supportive network of friends who were constantly there for me. I talked to other mothers who had gone through similar experiences with their babies. I spent time in quiet meditation to calm myself. I read everything I could on my daughter's prognosis, because then, as today, I believed knowledge is power. Finally, I spent time in nature, often running, which helped me stay as grounded.

I know that when I have something totally unexpected show up, I have to utilize additional tools and strategies to keep from becoming completely derailed. One of the things I do daily is a quiet meditation. In times of extreme duress I might do my meditation for a longer period of time or several times a day. For some people this could include prayer, deep breathing, chanting, or singing.

Another strategy I use is to call someone from my support team for a conversation. This can really help with gaining perspective, feeling heard, and regaining a sense of balance. Life is not fair; sometimes the unexpected challenges that show up can feel unbearable. In my experience, the strategies I have described can make a world of difference.

It is important to have solutions for dealing with daily adversity that come from a place of power and patience. By developing a plan to keep handy in your backpack, you will have created a tool for successfully and agilely maneuvering around any obstacle that you find in your path. One day at a time. Practice and keep moving forward. The summit is in sight.

Chapter Sixteen Exercises

Call to Action: Daily Adversity

1. How do you currently handle adversity in your everyday life? Examine your style of moving through obstacles. Do you procrastinate? Do you bulldoze through it? Do you ignore it? Do you engage in distractions, such as television, food, alcohol? Do you explode in anger?

2. What behaviors do you need to incorporate to successfully handle the smaller obstacles in life? Write down some steps to take and begin implementing those behaviors today to strengthen your capacity to handle larger adversities.

3. Make a list of known obstacles and possible adversities you will face in accomplishing your goal. Create a plan. Write down how you will handle the hardships.

4. What can you do if you encounter a hardship that is completely unexpected and unplanned for? What will help you move through the unidentified adversity that can present?

17 | Notice the Views Along the Way

"Enjoy the journey, enjoy every moment, and quit worrying about winning and losing."
—Matt Biondi, Olympic swimmer

I can vividly remember my first trekking experience in Nepal, when I was preparing to climb Mount Everest. By this time one person in our climbing party had already dropped out leaving twelve of us plus our expedition advisor. Tension was building. I could feel a competitive energy welling up inside of me, matching the spirited vigor within the group. Each day was filled with who would be first, who was best, and who would beat whom. Who would be the first to arrive at the tea house on our daily hikes? How was everyone adjusting to the altitude? Who had the best climbing stories? Who had the most technical experience? Rivalry became consuming.

Competition had me in its grip. I refused to be viewed as the weak link, so every day I hiked with the fastest group, racing to our next destination. This went on until the altitude stopped me in my tracks at 20,500 feet. We were hiking toward Advanced Base Camp, which is at the altitude of 21,000 feet. Only 500 feet from camp I was suddenly hit with the feeling that I had been hit by a truck, a very large truck. I was left breathless and exhausted. I realized that with aggressive competition I would be severely challenged to meet my goal.

This experience taught me that in the end there is no benefit to racing ahead. The final destination, the summit, was accomplished not by going as fast as possible, but by moving at a pace that allowed my body to acclimate properly. I was humbled by this newfound awareness.

My history was to live a fast-paced life, rushing through my experiences and skipping the views along the way. I would fixate on the desired outcome, put my blinders on, and go for it. It was as though my running shoes were always on, the bike was ready to go, and my adrenals never rested but were always ready for the next rush. I was on fast forward. I felt a need to live at that velocity in every area of my life. By doing so, I now realize that I have missed a lot of joy, beauty, and opportunities along the way.

Learning to slow down has offered me the opportunity to experience and see more enjoyment seeping into my life. Moving at a slower pace, I have discovered a simpler way of being. This allows me to notice opportunities along the way that I would have missed in my previous rush to accomplish the next thing. A more leisurely tempo encourages me to breathe, to appreciate my life so much more, and to enjoy the views, both from an inner perspective and a physical one as well. As I walk on trails or look out airplane windows I have a much different approach than in the past.

Staying in the present, with greater awareness of

everything around me, and moving at a slower pace has also shifted my mountain guiding experiences. I returned to Nepal a few years after summiting Mount Everest as a guide. This time I did not rush ahead. I was calm and at peace with a slower rate, lingering over meals at the tea houses and enjoying our rest days, some with and some without day hikes. Even waiting for weather windows became a pleasant experience for me.

I fully enjoyed the new tempo that allowed me to experience, with all of my senses, the magnificent mountain views, the villages, the people, and the Nepali culture. I walked away from that incident feeling enriched and alive, savoring the full experience. It was very freeing to focus on the whole experience in the moment rather than viewing the end result with blinders on.

As you can see, there can be a tendency to get so fixated on the end result that the enjoyment of the process is lost. I was one of those people until I had a chance to reflect on how I actually managed to reach the summit and then to return to Base Camp and ultimately to home safely. In the end, I was able to appreciate what really mattered. I have come to understand that the entire process—from making the decision to climb Mount Everest, to training, to the actual climb, to returning home, to what I am sharing with the world now—was as important as standing on the summit.

Accomplishing any goal that you set out to achieve is incredibly valuable. I challenge you to be aware of the whole process and enjoy the scenery along the way. Experience the rugged terrain, peaceful valleys, the joy, and the splendor. Notice the nagging mind chatter, unrelenting doubt, and criticisms without judgment. Observe the colors, sights, sounds, and textures of the interior and exterior world as you take each step. It is all part of the journey, and the whole of the process is as valuable and every bit as powerful as the accomplishment of the goal.

Chapter Seventeen Exercises

Call to Action: Notice the Views along the Way

1. Think of one goal that you have accomplished in your life that was a powerful experience for you. How did you travel that journey? Did you rush through it? Did you burn yourself out? Did you savor the experience?

2. What would have made the achievement of that goal more enjoyable?

3. Write down three lessons you learned in the achievement of that goal. How can this awareness fuel the success of your next goal?

18 | You've Climbed Your Everest— Now What?

"What you get by achieving your goals is as important as what you become."
—Zig Zigler, *What I Learned on My Way to the Top*

When I returned from the Mount Everest expedition, I remember feeling lost. I was also feeling some symptoms of depression, loss, lack of direction, and lack of focus. So much time, energy, and focus had been specifically directed towards accomplishing my big goal that without the focus I felt out of balance. What could possibly top standing on the pinnacle of the world? I knew I would need to consider what was next; yet I was unsure of how to change gears. I share this with you because once you have accomplished your goal you may experience some of these same feelings. I have come to accept this as part of the process. In fact, having a chance to evaluate what would come next changed my life from being "me" focused to a more outward perspective, with my energy being channeled towards relationships with others, family, and career.

Here is an email recap of my experience that I sent; it truly sums up this point. I wrote it as soon as I got down to Advanced Base Camp after the summit:

"Hi all, I just wanted to drop a line to let everyone know that I am down safely from the summit of Everest and am in ABC. It is the first safe place below the summit push and can take a while to get here after a summit, as you are so tired, and the weather can play a part in how quickly you are able to descend. I feel very lucky to have had the chance to summit in nice weather (for Everest) with no problems. The mountain was very gracious to me. Just a quick note on summit day; the route is very dangerous and scary. Without the help and encouragement of my Sherpa, it would have been a very sketchy thing for me to do. I knew it would be hard, but I could never have imagined. I kept thinking of all the support I have received for this climb, which I drew on when I was scared or tired. Thanks to you all for being such great support. I needed this for the climb. It pushed me beyond what I thought I was capable of. I am looking forward to the journey home at this point. It is time to reconnect with my family and friends. Love Laurie.

I have often wondered about the people who died on Mount Everest. Was it possible that their lives were so wrapped up in achieving the summit that once they reached the goal there was no reason to live? Sad, but true, some people die because they don't feel like they can do anything bigger, harder, or more fulfilling than what they have accomplished. Their purpose for living is gone.

I discovered that I was clearly not the same person when I returned home. Things that used to matter to me no longer did. Relationships changed; some deepened and some ended. My divorce became final, and I sold my half of our business to my ex-husband. After selling my business I had to reinvent myself with a new career. I not only finalized the completion of the marriage, I entered a new relationship with the love of my life. Everything was brand new. Everything had changed. Be prepared for some life-changing shifts yourself as you move into new territory, having done what you set out to do.

I recognize that my ability to summit was a gift. Only 10 percent of the climbers who attempt the summit—excluding guides, Sherpas, or expedition advisors—actually succeed. There had to be a specific reason that I was allowed to be in that 10 percent. I began to look for deeper meaning and purpose related to my experience. After taking the time to look at the bigger picture, I came to the conclusion that sharing my process with others and assisting them in achieving their goals would be the greatest gift of all.

I began to work on creating and teaching a goal-setting practice methodology. It became a thrilling prospect for me to share, motivate, and inspire people to move forward in their lives and actualize their dreams. Since I was not the most likely candidate to summit Mount Everest I had to work with discipline, dedication, commitment, and a plan to succeed. Along the way I acquired the tools necessary for success. The techniques for succeeding in any practice are a tried and true plan that will work for any goal, large or small. Another truth I learned was that without passion, burning passion, most goals will not endure the process it takes to accomplish them.

To start my process of answering the "now what" question, I first took all the time necessary to reflect, review, and evaluate the journey I had completed. I looked at what worked, what did not work, the things I would have done differently, and what I would do in the same manner. I wrote down the lessons I learned by viewing the expedition from my personal inside experience as well as from the outside experience. I also acknowledged that what might have been important to me while accomplishing this goal may no longer motivate or inspire me for future endeavors.

This review helped me gain a better understanding of the importance of every nuance of the journey. With this new-found wisdom as an integral part of me, I am now able to approach new goals in a healthier, holistic manner.

As you begin your journey of answering the question, "What's next?" take the time to slow down and review what you have already accomplished. Begin to make a plan that incorporates the wisdom you have acquired. Stick to your plan and be ready with a Plan B in your pack. Know you will encounter adversity and be prepared. Be ready and open to acknowledge what you have learned and how you may have changed because of it.

Chapter Eighteen Exercises

Call to Action: You've Climbed Your Everest—
Now What?

1. What is the biggest goal you have achieved in your
    life? Take time to review all the nuances of that
    journey and write down the most important.

2. How do you feel about the journey as a whole?
    How do you feel about how you participated in the
    journey? What wisdom did you acquire from your
    success?

3. Thinking about your next step with the wisdom you
    have gained, begin to make a plan for accomplish-
    ing your new big goal.

19 | Adventuring into New Realms

"'Come to the cliff,' he said.
They said, 'No we are afraid.'
'Come to the cliff,' he said.
They came.
He pushed them.
They flew!"
—Stuart Wilde, *The Warrior's Wisdom*

Once I had climbed Mount Everest, I no longer felt a pull toward high altitude mountaineering. Even though I have done a fair amount of guiding since my return, I have chosen mountains that were physically challenging but technically straightforward. I recognized that my goals focusing on competing no longer had a charge for me. I desired to gather all of my learned experiences and take them into the world to serve humanity in a new way, a way that is not self-focused but rather people-serving.

It took two years after I returned home from Nepal before I actually determined what was next for me. I tried several paths that felt sort of right, but not quite. After entertaining these new choices and doing a great deal of searching, I finally created a plan for myself that felt inspiring, motivating, and worthwhile.

I have learned to recognize that when something is not moving forward, despite my efforts, it is time to rethink my plan. Perhaps it was the wrong goal for me; maybe the timing just wasn't right for the goal. Maybe I need to revisit the goal (or not) at a different point in my life. Perhaps it was just going to take longer than I had hoped to complete my new goal. I remind myself to remember the journey and to be content with where I am as opposed to constantly wanting to be further along the path or even at the destination.

The energy I had used for training to climb Mount Everest went into reinventing myself. I put my focus into creating a new career, parenting my daughter, and nurturing my new love relationship. My enthusiasm for goal setting and achievement kept me focused on developing my skills and knowledge base; it helped me continue working on incorporating them into personal and business development. I am devoted to this work and feel it is perfect venue to assist people in realizing their dreams.

When you take the leap of faith and plunge into the journey that moves you towards accomplishing your big goal, you will discover many things about yourself. Some of these insights happen immediately, and others come with hindsight. You will also become aware of how you responded to reaching the goal that you invested so much time and energy into accomplishing. It is important to gather this information, because it will assist you in evaluating your "what's next."

How do we navigate new territory? What does it take to step out of our comfort zones and into the unknown? First, recognize that you have had many firsts in life; the first day of school, the first date, the first job, a career change, and the accomplishment of goals. It all started with the unknown, new terrain. Recognizing the hundreds of firsts in life eases the resistance to begin something new.

By following the steps throughout this book you will find a road map to dream into the next grand adventure. It will assist you to make the decision to go for it, establish goals, and implement the action plan to attain them. Remember the beginning of the last goal you achieved. Do you remember the excitement? To begin again is to enter the power of that excitement. As you have discovered throughout this journey, goals are realized one day at a time. Sometimes the steps are baby steps and sometimes they are quantum leaps. I know of no other way to jump off the cliff than to take a leap of faith and jump!

20 | Putting It All Together—Your Life Purpose

"The interdependency of human kind, the relevance of relationship, the sacredness of creation is ancient wisdom."
—Rebecca Adamson, *Land Rich and Dirt Poor*

How do you decide what your life purpose is? People can spend their entire lives on this question. I admit it has been a forty-six year process for me as well. The good news is there are some tools and strategies that can speed this process. One idea is to examine what you're good at and passionate about, and then to explore how you can use these two elements to help our world. This could mean making a difference for mankind, the environment, or the animals of the world.

It took me hours of meditation, journaling, conversation, and feedback from trusted mentors and friends before I got clear on what my next mountain would be and what that bigger picture looked like. When I explore my definition of a universal goal what comes to mind is the desire to collaborate with others in a way that supports and improves our planet and the lives of others.

One experience relevant to this happened recently. I was at the Nordic center getting ready for a leisurely skate ski when I noticed a group gathered at what looked like a starting line. I realized that they were just about to start a race. As the gun went off, a few people in snow shoes raced up the trail for a 6.2-mile snow-shoe race.

A few years ago this would have been right up my alley. The idea of pushing myself physically and being pitted against other people would have been highly mo-tivating. About halfway through the race, as I was skat-ing along, I saw the racers coming up the hill, sweating, grimacing, panting, and straining with every muscle in their bodies, which showed on people's faces. Not one person looked like they were enjoying themselves.

I remember thinking to myself that I am so glad I am not driven by this need anymore. It looks painful and unpleasant to say the least. Even though my gifts re-main the same, the ways I want to use them are now different. As you explore the possibility of moving to-wards a universal goal, you may find the same trans-formation. What used to be motivating and inspiring has changed.

Discovering one's gifts and passions can be difficult for some to do and easy for others. Once you have done the work of figuring this out, the next step is to put this information to work so that it supports you and enhances the earth and the lives of others.

To review, at this point you have identified your dream. You have looked at your strengths and gifts and have written down a goal or goals that inspire and motivate you. You have begun the process of developing a plan. Many goals have more than one component to develop. Your plan should reflect your unique needs. Furthermore, you have the opportunity to decide if you want to accomplish your goal and at the same time make a difference for someone or something else. You have learned how to increase your confidence, which will benefit you in all areas of your life.

We have explored the importance of keeping options open and staying flexible since what we want may take a different form than we had originally imagined. Never underestimate the power of a commitment to yourself, and better yet make a personal pledge to solidify this commitment.

As you move forward it is crucial to honestly evaluate your abilities to obtain your goal. I use an "A to Z" scale and place myself where I think I currently am, knowing that this will set the stage for getting to "Z." Looking at your current habits and deciding if they are supporting your forward progress is an important step. This includes developing an awareness of your current pace and the degree to which it is serving you.

There are many options for tools that solidify habits. You will need to decide if affirmations, visualizations, or quotes inspire you. You will need to explore sources of helpful information such as books, trainings, or other media, like CDs and DVDs. Never forget the power of concentrated focus. It is an item you should always keep in your pack. I also cannot stress enough the importance of having a support team that includes a coach or mentor who has done what you want to do. In addition, having others on your team who are solid in their belief in you will create a spirit of teamwork and community.

Keep in mind Doug Carter's maxim, "All you ever have to do is take the next step." This action step maintains focus and momentum. As we discussed, you may encounter storms, red flags, and daily adversity. How you handle the unexpected hardships and challenges that require decisions and create daily stress will make your journey more joyous. The action step that I use is to be as prepared as possible. This may require anticipating what could go wrong, giving yourself some time before reacting, and having a Plan B in the event your intended steps are derailed. Lastly, as you move forward, don't miss the joyful moments. Enjoy the entire process. This alone will make the next steps much easier to navigate. Eventually you will come to the "Now what?" question, and this will propel you into evaluating what your new realm looks like.

Everything I have talked about in this book, all the steps that I have outlined, are more than possible for you. Though the ideas, tools, and strategies sound simple there is often nothing easy about accomplishing a dream. I encourage you to work with the steps, create a plan, and as you venture forward, redefine your path as needed. It will be important to revise when you are called to. Vow to enjoy your journey and breathe deeply as you make a difference for yourself and others. Take this life and run with it! It is a choice you will not regret.

Laurie Bagley— Workshops and Coaching

Laurie Bagley is available to facilitate workshops and seminars; in addition, she offers her own unique approach to long-distance fitness coaching.

- To learn more about Laurie Bagley's workshop: "Journey to the Summit. Goal Setting One Step at a Time," go to www.LaurieBagley.com. There you will also learn about her availability for remote fitness coaching, speaking, and seminar facilitation and leadership.

- More information on this book or related products is available online at www.SummitEverestBook.com.

Praise for Laurie Bagley

"Laurie's story of her successful summit inspired me to develop my personal powers of setting clear goals, taking focused action and persevering one step at a time!"
—**Kathy Hall**, Starlight Productions, Mount Shasta, California

"I have twice attended your Jedi Goal Workshops, and once your Everest presentation. While I have long enjoyed my career passions for animals and healing, the inspiration for compiling and sharing these many worthwhile stories in a book or audio eluded me. One day recently, it just clicked, and I more deeply understood what it means, as you say, to be alive with the fire of purpose. As I work now near the completion of the first e-book, I am appreciating the way you taught us to stay present with the very next step, however small, and to stay focused with faith that our training and experience will see us through to where we envision."
—**Winterhawk,** Winterhawk Animal Consultations